CAMBRIDGE LIBRARY COLLECTION

Books of enduring scholarly value

Archaeology

The discovery of material remains from the recent or the ancient past has always been a source of fascination, but the development of archaeology as an academic discipline which interpreted such finds is relatively recent. It was the work of Winckelmann at Pompeii in the 1760s which first revealed the potential of systematic excavation to scholars and the wider public. Pioneering figures of the nineteenth century such as Schliemann, Layard and Petrie transformed archaeology from a search for ancient artifacts, by means as crude as using gunpowder to break into a tomb, to a science which drew from a wide range of disciplines - ancient languages and literature, geology, chemistry, social history - to increase our understanding of human life and society in the remote past.

A Primer of Assyriology

Archibald Henry Sayce (1845–1933) became interested in Middle Eastern languages and scripts while still a teenager. Old Persian and Akkadian cuneiform had recently been deciphered, and popular enthusiasm for these discoveries was running high when Sayce began his academic career at Oxford in 1869. This 1894 work, published by the Religious Tract Society, is an introduction for a popular readership to the world of ancient Assyria. Beginning with the geography of Mesopotamia and with the early archaeological discoveries in the region, Sayce next describes the decipherment of the cuneiform inscriptions and tablets, and the knowledge gained from them, especially about the history of the region, and government and organisation, before describing religion, literature, and what can be deduced about everyday life. An appendix gives weights and measures, lists of kings and gods, and a chronological table linking events known from the archaeological record to accounts in the Old Testament.

Cambridge University Press has long been a pioneer in the reissuing of out-of-print titles from its own backlist, producing digital reprints of books that are still sought after by scholars and students but could not be reprinted economically using traditional technology. The Cambridge Library Collection extends this activity to a wider range of books which are still of importance to researchers and professionals, either for the source material they contain, or as landmarks in the history of their academic discipline.

Drawing from the world-renowned collections in the Cambridge University Library and other partner libraries, and guided by the advice of experts in each subject area, Cambridge University Press is using state-of-the-art scanning machines in its own Printing House to capture the content of each book selected for inclusion. The files are processed to give a consistently clear, crisp image, and the books finished to the high quality standard for which the Press is recognised around the world. The latest print-on-demand technology ensures that the books will remain available indefinitely, and that orders for single or multiple copies can quickly be supplied.

The Cambridge Library Collection brings back to life books of enduring scholarly value (including out-of-copyright works originally issued by other publishers) across a wide range of disciplines in the humanities and social sciences and in science and technology.

A Primer of Assyriology

ARCHIBALD HENRY SAYCE

CAMBRIDGE
UNIVERSITY PRESS

CAMBRIDGE
UNIVERSITY PRESS

University Printing House, Cambridge, CB2 8BS, United Kingdom

Cambridge University Press is part of the University of Cambridge.
It furthers the University's mission by disseminating knowledge in the pursuit of
education, learning and research at the highest international levels of excellence.

www.cambridge.org
Information on this title: www.cambridge.org/9781108082341

© in this compilation Cambridge University Press 2015

This edition first published 1894
This digitally printed version 2015

ISBN 978-1-108-08234-1 Paperback

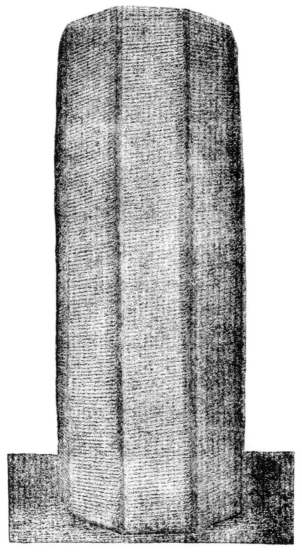

CLAY CYLINDER OF TIGLATH-PILESER I.

Present Day Primers

A

Primer of Assyriology

BY

A. H. SAYCE, LL.D.

PROFESSOR OF ASSYRIOLOGY, OXFORD
AUTHOR OF 'FRESH LIGHT FROM THE ANCIENT MONUMENTS'
'ASSYRIA, ITS PRINCES, PRIESTS, AND PEOPLE,' ETC.

WITH SEVEN ILLUSTRATIONS

THE RELIGIOUS TRACT SOCIETY

56 PATERNOSTER ROW AND 65 ST. PAUL'S CHURCHYARD

First Edition, September, 1894.

CONTENTS

—✦✦—

CHAPTER I

THE COUNTRY AND ITS PEOPLE

CHAPTER II

THE DISCOVERY AND DECIPHERMENT OF THE INSCRIPTIONS

CHAPTER III

BABYLONIAN AND ASSYRIAN HISTORY

6 *CONTENTS*

CHAPTER IV

RELIGION

PAGE

The religions of Babylonia and Assyria — Differences
between Babylonian and Assyrian religion—Sumerian
religion Shamanistic — Two centres of Babylonian
religion—Semitic influence—The goddess Istar—Bel-
Merodach—Other deities—Sacred books and ritual—
The Priests—The Temples—Astro-theology—Sacrifices and offerings — The Sabbath — Monotheistic
tendency—The future life—Cosmology .   .   . 80

CHAPTER V

BABYLONIAN AND ASSYRIAN LITERATURE

Aids to the reading of the texts—The libraries—Varieties
of literature — The texts autotypes — Astronomy—
Mathematics—Medicine and law—History and mythology—The Chaldaean epic and the Deluge—Epic
of the Creation 95

CHAPTER VI

SOCIAL LIFE

The Contract-tablets—Married Life—Burial—Slavery—
Lowness of Wages—Property—Taxes—Prices—Usury
—The Army—Navy—The Bureaucracy .   .   . 109

APPENDIX

Assyrian Measures of Length—Measures of Capacity—
Measures of Weight and Coinage—The Months of the
Year 118

Babylonian Kings—Assyrian Kings—High Priests of Assur
—Kings of Assyria 120

Synchronisms between Assyrian and Biblical History   . 125

The Principal Deities of Babylonia and Assyria   .   . 126

A PRIMER OF ASSYRIOLOGY

CHAPTER I

THE COUNTRY AND ITS PEOPLE

Geography.—The civilizations of Babylonia and Assyria grew up on the banks of the Tigris and Euphrates. The Tigris was called Idikna and Idikla in the Sumerian or primitive language of Babylonia, from which the Semites formed the name Idiklat, by means of the feminine suffix -*t*. In later times the name was shortened into Diklat, and finally assimilated by the Persians to the word Tigra, which in their language signified 'an arrow.' It is from Tigra that the classical name Tigris is derived. In Genesis (ii. 14), however, the ancient name Idikla, there written Hiddekel, is still preserved. The Euphrates was called Pura-nun, or 'great water,' in Sumerian, and was frequently known as simply the Pura or 'Water,' just as the Nile is known to-day to the modern Egyptians as simply 'the Sea.' Hence it is often spoken of in the Bible as 'the River,' without the addition of any other name. From Pura came the Semitic Purat, with the Semitic suffix -*t*; and Purat, the Perath of the Old Testament, was changed by the Persians into Ufratu, with a play upon their own word *u* 'good.' The Persian Ufratu is the Greek Euphrates.

The alluvial plain of Babylonia was the gift of the two great rivers. In the early days of Babylonian civilization they both flowed into the Persian Gulf. But salt marshes already existed at their mouths, and as time went on the marshes extended further and further to the south. What had once been sea became dry land, the silt brought down by the rivers forming an ever-increasing delta in the north of the Gulf. To-day the two rivers flow into one channel, and the point where they unite is eighty miles distant from the present line of coast. The marshes are called 'the country of Marratu' or 'the salt-sea' in the inscriptions, a name which reappears as Merathaim in Jer. l. 21.

One of the oldest of Babylonian cities was Eridu, 'the good city,' which was originally built on the shore of the Persian Gulf, though Abu-Shahrein, which now marks its site, is far inland, the sea having retreated from it for a distance of 100 miles. In early times, however, it was the chief Babylonian port, and through its intercourse with foreign countries it exercised a great influence on the culture and religion of Babylonia. Further to the north, but on the western side of the Euphrates, was Ur, the birth-place of Abraham, whose ruins are now called Mugheir or Muqayyar; and still further to the north, but on the opposite side of the river, were Larsa (probably the Ellasar of Gen. xiv. 1) now Senkereh, and Uruk or Erech (Gen. x. 10) the modern Warka. Considerably to the north of these again came Nipur (now Niffer), which played a leading part in the history of Babylonian religion. Nipur stood at the spot where the Tigris and Euphrates tended to approach one another, and northward, in the narrowest part of the territory which lay between them, were the important cities of Babel or Babylon, Kutha, and Sippara. Babylon, called Bab-ili, 'the gate of God,' on the monuments, lay on both sides of the Euphrates, its south-western suburb being Borsippa. The great temple of Bel-Merodach, called Ê-Saggila, rose within it; that of Nebo, the prophet and interpreter of Merodach, being at Borsippa.

Ê-Zida, the temple of Nebo, is now known as the Birs-i-Nimrûd. Kutha (now Tell-Ibrahim), to the north of Babylon, was surrounded by vast cemeteries, which were under the protection of its patron-god Nergal. Sippara, still further to the north, was a double city, one part of it, the present Abu-Habba, being termed 'Sippara of the Sun-god,' while the other half was 'Sippara of the goddess Anunit.' It is in consequence of this double character that the Old Testament speaks of it as Sepharvaim 'the two Sipparas.'

Northward of Sippara the Tigris and Euphrates again trend apart from one another and enclose the great plateau of Mesopotamia. To the east of the Tigris come the mountains of Elam, 'the highlands,' and to the north of them the Kurdish ranges, which were known to the primitive Babylonians under the name of Guti or Gutium. At the foot of these ranges, and northward of the Lower or Little Zab, the kingdom of Assyria arose. It took its name from its original capital of Assur, now Kalah-Sherghat, on the western bank of the Tigris, not far to the north of the junction of the latter river with the Lower Zab. The supremacy of Assur afterwards passed to Calah and Nineveh, which lay northward between the Tigris and the Upper or Greater Zab. Calah (now Nimrûd) was close to the junction of the two rivers; Nineveh (now Kouyunjik and Nebi Yunus opposite Mosul) was built along the bank of the Tigris, the stream of the Khoser flowing through the middle of it. Some miles to the north, under the shelter of the hills, Sargon built a palace which he called Dur-Sargon (the modern Khorsabad), and between Nineveh and Calah lay Res-eni 'the head of the Spring,' the Resen of Gen. x. 12.

Population and Language.—Babylonia already had a long history behind it when the kingdom of Assyria first arose. The main bulk of the Assyrian population was Semitic, and the common language of the country was Semitic also. But it was otherwise in Babylonia. Here the pioneers of civilization, the builders of the great cities, the inventors of the cuneiform system of writing, of astronomy, of mathematics, and of other arts and sciences, belonged to a non-Semitic race and spoke an agglutinative language. It is in this language that the earliest records of the country are written and that the older clay-books were compiled. For want of a better name scholars have called the language and people to whom it belonged

Accadian or Sumerian, or even Accado-Sumerian. Accad and Sumer were the names given to the northern and southern divisions of Babylonia respectively, and as it was in Sumer that the old race and language lingered the longest, 'Sumerian' would appear to be the best title to apply to them. Indeed it is possible that the city of Agade or Accad, from which the district of Accad seems to have derived its name, was of Semitic foundation. In any case the Semitic element in Accad was from very early times stronger than that in Sumer, and consequently the Sumerian dialect spoken in the north was more largely affected by Semitic influence and the resulting phonetic decay than was the dialect spoken in the south. Sumerian was agglutinative, like the languages of the modern Finns or Turks, the relations of grammar being expressed by suffixes (or prefixes) which retain an independent meaning of their own. Thus *dingir* is 'god,' *dingir-ene* 'gods,' *dingir-ene-ku* 'to the gods;' *mu-ru* 'I built,' *mu-na-ru* 'I built it.'

The Semitic dialects of Babylonia and Assyria differed very slightly from one another, and they are therefore called by the common name of Assyrian. We can trace the history of Assyrian by means of contemporaneous monuments for nearly 4,000 years,

beginning with the records of Sargon of Accad
(B. C. 3800) and ending with documents of the Par-
thian epoch. Assyrian belongs to the northern group
of Semitic languages, being more closely related to
Hebrew and Aramaic than it is to Arabic or Ethiopic.

The Chaldaeans.—When the Semites first obtained political power in Babylonia we do not know.
The earliest Semitic empire known to us is that of
Sargon of Accad. Babylon did not become the
capital of a united kingdom till much later, Khammurabi (B. C. 2350) being apparently the first who
made it so. Strictly speaking, it is only after this
event that the name of 'Babylonia' is applicable to
the whole country. In the Old Testament the Babylonians are called Kasdim, a word of uncertain origin.
It is rendered 'Chaldaeans' in the Authorized Version; the classical Chaldaeans, however, took their
name from the Kaldâ, a tribe settled in the salt-
marshes, of whom we first hear in an inscription of
the twelfth century B. C. One of their princes was
Merodach-baladan (Isaiah xxxix) who made himself
master of all Babylonia. It is probable that Nebuchadrezzar was also of Kaldâ descent. After the
time of Merodach-baladan the Kaldâ formed so in-

tegral a part of the population as to give their name
to the whole of it in the writings of the Greeks and
Romans, and after the fall of Babylonia, when Babylonian astrologers and fortune-tellers made their way
to the west, 'Chaldaean' became synonymous with
'diviner.'

The Kassi.—Another element in the Babylonian
population consisted of the Kassi (the Kossaeans or
Kissians of the Greeks), who came from the mountains
of Elam.   They spoke originally a non-Semitic language, and gave a dynasty of kings to Babylonia
which lasted 576 years and nine months.   The
dynasty was reigning in the century before the Exodus
when the cuneiform tablets of Tel el-Amarna were
written, and we learn from them that the Babylonians
were at that time called Kassi (or Kasi) in Canaan.

Natural Products.—The soil of Babylonia was
exceedingly fertile.   It was the natural home of the
wheat which still grows wild in the neighbourhood of
Anah.   Herodotus tells us that 'the leaf of the wheat
and barley is as much as four fingers in width, and
the stalks of the millet and sesame are so tall that no
one who has never been in that country would believe

me were I to mention their height.' It was calculated
that grain produced on an average a return of two
hundred for one on the seed sown, the return in
favourable seasons being as much as three hundred.
The chief tree of the country was the palm. Prices
were frequently calculated in corn and dates, and the
dates among other uses served to make wine. Though
vines seem to have been grown, most of the grape-
wine drunk in the country was imported from abroad.

Canals.—The whole country was intersected by
canals, and carefully irrigated by means of machines.
The canals thus regulated the supply of water and
enabled it to be carried beyond the reach of the
rivers. The two principal canals were called the
Nahar-Malcha or Royal River and the Pallacopas
(Pallukat in the inscriptions).

Architecture.—Babylonia was devoid of stone,
which had to be brought from the mountains of Elam
or elsewhere. In this respect it offered a striking
contrast to Assyria, where good stone was plentiful.
To this absence of stone may be traced some of the
peculiarities of its early culture. It caused clay to
become the common writing material of the country,

the cuneiform characters being impressed with a stylus upon the tablet while the clay was still moist. It further obliged every building to be of brick. This led to a great development of columnar architecture, the wooden columns which supported the roof being subsequently imitated in brick. The use of brick further led to the use of stucco and painting. The walls of the Chaldaean houses, as we learn from Ezekiel (xxiii. 14), were decorated with ' images pourtrayed with vermilion,' unlike those of the Assyrian palaces which were lined with slabs of sculptured alabaster. Assyrian art was, however, borrowed from that of Babylonia ; hence the colouration of the Assyrian bas-reliefs on stone ; hence also the great mounds on which the Assyrian palaces were built. Such mounds were needful in the flat country of Babylonia where inundations were frequent; in Assyria they were not required.

Asphalt and Naphtha.—Besides clay, Babylonia also furnishes asphalt and naphtha. According to Poseidonios the naphtha was partly white, partly black, the latter being that which was used for lamps. Naphtha is still found near Hit, 130 miles to the north of Babylon.

Character of the Babylonians and Assyrians.
—The contrast between the physical characteristics of Babylonia and Assyria was paralleled by a contrast between the characters of their inhabitants. The population of Babylonia was pre-eminently agricultural and peaceable, that of Assyria pre-eminently military. Babylonia was the land of letters; in Assyria the power to read and write was mainly confined to the scribes. Both Babylonians and Assyrians, however, were keen traders and merchants, but while 'the cry of the Chaldaeans was in their ships,' the Assyrians had no taste for the sea. The Babylonians seem to have been a gentler people, more pious and superstitious; the Assyrians, on the other hand, had a genius for organization and administrative work. Such differences may be traced as much to a difference in the conditions under which they lived as to a difference in race.

CHAPTER II

The Site of Babylon.—The site of Babylon was
never forgotten. In the twelfth century, Benjamin
of Tudela describes the ruins of Nebuchadrezzar's
palace which he saw there, and in 1573 the English
traveller Eldred visited the spot, and found the
Tower of Babel in the Birs-i-Nimrûd, which he states
to be a mile in circumference and about as high as
St. Paul's Cathedral. Other travellers have left
notices of the ruins. But the first to explore them
scientifically was Rich, the Resident of the East
India Company at Bagdad, who surveyed and made
a map of them. His work on the site of the old city
was published in 1811. But it was not until 1850
that the first excavations were made by Sir A. H.
Layard, which were followed in 1851–4 by the

French expedition under Fresnel, Thomas, and Oppert. The fruit of the expedition was an elaborate memoir by Oppert, which marks an epoch in the history of cuneiform decipherment, and determined the ancient topography of Babylon. The excavations were resumed by Sir H. Rawlinson in 1854, who discovered the architectural records of Nebuchadrezzar, at the same time that other ancient sites of Babylonian civilization were being excavated by Loftus and Taylor. At a much later period (in 1879 and 1882) the work of excavation was again taken up by Mr. Hormuzd Rassam, who discovered the site of Sippara, and disinterred the ancient temple there of the Sun-god. Equally important were the discoveries made by the French consul, M. de Sarzec, in 1877–81 at Tello (the ancient Lagas) in southern Chaldaea. Monuments of the early Sumerian period of Babylonian history were brought to light, including seated statues and bas-reliefs, which are now in the Museum of the Louvre.

The Site of Nineveh.—The identification of Nineveh was less easy than that of Babylon. Its site was lost, although the natives of the district had not altogether forgotten the name of Nunia, and

Niebuhr in the last century, believed that it marked the site of the Assyrian capital[1]. But its real discovery was due to Rich. Shortly before his visit to Mosul a bas-relief had been found on the opposite side of the Tigris, which the Mohammedans had destroyed as being the work of the 'infidels.' His examination of the mounds from which it had come led to the discovery of walls and cuneiform inscriptions, which left no doubt in his mind that the site was that of Nineveh. He accordingly drew up a map of the ruins, which he sent to Europe along with his collection of Babylonian and Assyrian antiquities. A single case, three feet in diameter, was sufficient for their accommodation in the British Museum.

Excavations.—These antiquities, however, inspired the French *savant*, Mohl, with the conviction that if excavations were undertaken at the place where they had been found, important results would follow. Accordingly, he induced Botta, who had been sent as French Consul to Mosul in 1842, to commence digging there the following year. Botta

[1] In Dapper's *Circumstantial Description of Asia*, it is stated that opposite Mosul is 'a little town called up to the present day by Arab writers Nennouwi, and by the Turks Eski Mosul,' or Old Mosul.

was led by a native to the mound of Khorsabad, and his labours were soon rewarded by the discovery of Assyrian sculptures covered with cuneiform writing. The French government granted funds for the continuation of the work, and before 1845 the palace of Sargon was laid bare.

Meanwhile Layard had arrived on the spot, and with the help of funds principally supplied by Sir Stratford Canning, had opened trenches in the mound of Nimrûd (the ancient Calah). The spoils of the palaces he found here were transported to England in 1847. Among them was the famous Black Obelisk, on which mention is made of Jehu of Israel. At Kouyunjik also, among the ruins of the palaces of Sennacherib and Assur-bani-pal, excavations had been begun. But it was only after the return of Sir A. H. Layard to Mosul in 1849, with a grant from the British Museum, that a systematic exploration of this mound took place. Assisted by Mr. Hormuzd Rassam, he discovered here the libraries of clay books from which most of our knowledge of Assyria and Babylonia is derived. Excavations were further undertaken at Kalah Sherghat (the ancient Assur), where the records of Tiglath-pileser I were disinterred, in the ruined palaces of Sennacherib and

Esar-haddon at Nebi Yunus, at Arban on the Khabour (the ancient Sidikan), and at several other places. When the work was closed in 1852, a new world of art and literature had been revealed. Nothing further was done till the beginning of 1873, when George Smith was sent to Nineveh by the proprietors of the *Daily Telegraph* in order to search for the missing portions of the Deluge-tablet, and a year later he was again sent out to excavate by the British Museum. After his death, near Aleppo, in 1876, the excavations were entrusted to Mr. Hormuzd Rassam, who, in 1878, discovered the bronze gates of Balawât, and three years later the site of Sippara in Babylonia, as well as a library in the temple of its Sun-god. A similar library has since been discovered (in 1891) by the American expedition in the mounds of Niffer, where monuments of Sargon of Accad (B. C. 3800) have been brought to light.

The Decipherment of the Inscriptions.—The decipherment of the cuneiform texts has been one of the scientific triumphs of the present century. The key was given by the inscriptions on the ruined palaces and tombs of ancient Persia. Travellers at an early date had noticed these inscriptions at

Persepolis and elsewhere, and while some compared the forms of the characters composing them to arrows, others considered them to be wedges, *cunei* in Latin. The latter comparison was the origin of the term 'cuneiform,' ordinarily applied to them. We find it already used by Hyde in his *Historia Religionis veterum Persarum*, which was published at Oxford in 1700 [1].

The Italian traveller, Pietro della Valle, in 1621, was the first who made the characters known in Europe by printing a few of them; at the same time he put forward the correct suggestion that the inscriptions were to be read from left to right. A more important collection of signs, however, was published in 1693, in one of the early volumes (No. 201) of the *Philosophical Transactions* of the Royal Society from the papers of Mr. Flower, who had been specially charged by the East India Company with the duty of investigating the antiquities of Persia. But it was not till the middle of the eighteenth century that Cornelius van Bruyn (1714) and Carsten Niebuhr (1774-8), the father of the historian, first copied and published the inscriptions in anything like a complete and accurate manner. Niebuhr further pointed

---

[1] Hyde's words are 'ductuli pyramidales seu cuneiformes.'

out that they comprised three different systems of cuneiform writing, which in the case of every text followed one another in a regular order. The first system of writing was the simplest, as it consisted of only forty-two different characters, whereas the number of characters in the second and third systems was very large.

With Niebuhr's publication the work of decipherment became possible. In 1798, Professor Tychsen, of Rostock, discovered that in the first system an oblique wedge was used to divide the words from one another, and in 1802 the Danish Bishop, Münter, starting from this basis, showed that the language possessed suffixes, pointed out that certain characters denoted vowels, and even divined the word for 'king,' as well as the value of two letters, one of them being *a*. He also maintained that while the first system of writing was alphabetic, the second was syllabic, and the third ideographic, and that as the inscriptions were found in Persia and on the buildings of the Achaemenian kings, the text which always comes first must represent the language of ancient Persia, which he identified, though erroneously, with Zend.

It is, however, to George Frederick Grotefend,

of Hanover, that the discovery of the key which has unlocked the secrets of cuneiform literature is really due. On September 4, 1802, he read before the Royal Society of Göttingen a Memoir, in which he announced his discovery of the names of certain Achaemenian kings in the cuneiform inscriptions, and explained the method by which he had arrived at his results. By a curious coincidence it was at the same meeting of the Society that Heyne described the first efforts that had been made towards deciphering the Egyptian hieroglyphics. Grotefend first showed convincingly that the inscriptions must be read from left to right, a portion of a word which ends a line on the right side in one of the texts beginning the next line on the left side in a duplicate copy of it. He next pointed out that the analogy of the Sassanian inscriptions, which had just been deciphered by de Sacy, indicated that the Persepolitan texts must commence with the names of the kings who had erected the monuments, followed by their titles, and that a comparison of the texts one with another made it pretty evident that such was actually the case. In this way he succeeded in finding (like Münter before him) the word for 'king,' and in addition to this the royal names preceding it. Those on the Persepolitan

monuments represented a father and a son, though
in certain cases the father added his own father's
name, but without the royal titles.   Thanks to the
classical writers, it was known that the monuments
were of Achaemenian origin, and the names of the
Achaemenian kings had also been preserved.   It only
remained to fit them to the characters in the cuneiform texts.   Hystaspes, Darius, and Xerxes alone
suited, since Cyrus was too short and Artaxerxes too
long ; moreover, the letters *a*, *r*, and *sh*, in the names
of Darius and Xerxes appeared in their right places if
these names were adopted.   So, too, did *a* and *sh* in
the name of Hystaspes.   Such a coincidence was
sufficient to prove that Grotefend was right in his
guess that the words in question represented proper
names, for guess it was, though founded on strong
probability and scientific induction.   He had noticed
that two of the names (those of Darius and Xerxes)
occurred separately on two particular groups of
monuments, whereas the word which followed them
was always the same.   It was natural to conclude
that the latter word denoted 'king,' while those which
preceded it were proper names.

The alphabet Grotefend had constructed out of
the proper names enabled him to read the word for

'king,' and thus to show its near affinity to the corresponding word in Zend. But he was a classical scholar rather than an orientalist, better known by his Latin grammar than by his knowledge of Eastern languages, and consequently as soon as his pioneering work of decipherment was accomplished, he lacked the philological knowledge which would have allowed him to continue it. Moreover, he was hampered by the false theory that the language of the inscriptions was identical with Zend. The next step of importance was taken by Rask in 1826, who discovered the termination of the genitive plural and the true reading of the title 'Achaemenian.' Rask was followed in 1836 by the great Zendic scholar Burnouf at Paris, and by Lassen at Bonn. Burnouf demonstrated that the language of the Achaemenian texts was not Zend, but a sister dialect spoken in western Persia, and his discovery of the names of the satrapies, in one of the inscriptions copied by Niebuhr, enabled him and Lassen simultaneously almost to complete what we may henceforth call the Old Persian alphabet. A few corrections in it were subsequently made by Beer, Jacquet, Holzmann, and Lassen himself.

Meanwhile a young English officer in the East

India Company's service, now Sir Henry Rawlinson, had been working in Persia unassisted, and at a distance from libraries, upon the Old Persian texts. He knew that Grotefend had discovered in them the names of the early Achaemenian monarchs, and with this clue he set himself to construct an alphabet and interpret the inscriptions. He soon found means of providing himself with fuller materials for the work of decipherment than those at the disposal of scholars in Europe, by copying the great inscription which Darius had caused to be engraved on the sacred rock of Bagistana or Behistun in commemoration of his accession to the throne of Persia, and re-conquest of the empire of Cyrus. The task of copying the inscription—by far the longest Persian one known—was an arduous one, and not unattended with danger, and it occupied several years. Rawlinson first saw the inscription in 1835 ; it was not till 1839 that the whole of it was copied. A few years later he revised it again, but his memoir upon it and upon the other Old Persian texts was not ready for publication till 1845. In the following year the text was published by the Royal Asiatic Society, and the translation and commentary followed in 1849. Dr. Hincks, of Dublin, had already (in 1846) given the last touch to the decipherment of the Old Persian alphabet by the discovery that the consonants composing it contained inherent vowels.

As we have seen, Niebuhr had perceived that the Persepolitan inscriptions were in three different systems of writing. But it was only after the decipherment of the Persian texts that it was found that the three systems of writing embodied three separate languages, and belonged to three separate countries. As in modern Turkey a governor has to issue an edict in agglutinative Turkish, Semitic Arabic, and Aryan Persian, so too in ancient Persia a king who wished to be understood by all his subjects had to appeal to them in the Aryan language of Persian itself, in the Semitic language of Babylonia and Assyria, and in the agglutinative language of Susiania or Elam. When the second and third systems of writing came to be read it was discovered that the second contained the script and language of Elam—sometimes, but incorrectly, called Scythian, Medic or Protomedic, sometimes, more properly, Amardian or Neo-Susian—while the third was Babylonian. The three capitals of the empire, Persepolis, Susa and Babylon, were thus each of them represented.

The number of characters used in Amardian, though large, was limited, and accordingly, with the help of the proper names occurring in the Old Persian texts, a syllabary, or list of characters each expressing a syllable, was soon formed and the work of translation commenced. Westergaard, the Dane, who had already travelled in Persia, and there copied the inscription on the tomb of Darius at Naksh-i-Rustem, led the way in 1845. He was followed by Hincks, de Saulcy, and above all Edwin Norris, the learned Secretary of the Royal Asiatic Society, who published in 1853 the Amardian (or as he called it the ' Scythic ') version of the Behistun inscription, with an elaborate translation, commentary, and vocabulary. Further progress, in the study of the language was made by Oppert, whose book *Le Peuple et la Langue des Mèdes* (1879) is a monument of systematic research. Sayce's decipherment of the inscriptions of Mal-Amir, south-east of Susa, in 1884 (in the Proceedings of the Sixth Oriental Congress), showed that we must look to that part of Susiania for the origin of the Amardian syllabary and dialect. The language was, in fact, one of the agglutinative dialects spoken in Elam, the native language of Susa itself being closely related to it. Unfortunately, however, there is no known language with which the dialects of ancient Elam can be compared, and consequently our knowledge of them hardly extends beyond the help afforded by the trilingual Persian texts.

The decipherment of the third system of writing long seemed to baffle the inquirer. The characters were multitudinous, some of them were plainly ideographs, denoting ideas and not letters or syllables, while the same character did not always appear to have the same value. Moreover, the belief that the characters must represent alphabetic letters long stood in the way of the decipherer. Grotefend had already observed that they resembled in form the characters found on some of the antiquities which came from Babylonia, but it was not till after the excavation of Nineveh that any serious effort was made to decipher them. Botta and Layard, at the very outset, pointed out that the script used in Assyria was the same as that of the third Achaemenian system, and thus attracted fresh attention to the latter. Löwenstern was the first to attack the problem in 1845. His first essays, however, were unsuccessful, like those of de Saulcy in 1847, and his second publication (in 1847) did little more than establish the fact that the same name might be written with different signs. In the same year de Longpérier correctly deciphered the words and ideographs denoting 'palace,' 'king,' 'great,' and the like, though without being able to read phonetically any one of them. But in 1848 Botta published the numerous inscriptions he had discovered at Khorsabad, at the same time subjecting them to a careful analysis. He divided them into words, wherever it was possible, noting the variations in writing the same word, and drawing up a list of 642 classified characters. He further proved that the terminations or suffixes of words in the Assyrian texts agreed with those of the third Achaemenian system, an indication that the language was the same as well as the script. Finally he made it clear that the script contained not only phonetic characters, but also ideographs, and he correctly determined many of these ideographs, including that which denotes plurality. All that was now needed was to discover the phonetic equivalents of the characters.

This was done half a year later by de Saulcy, who analyzed the Babylonian transcript of the Achaemenian inscription at Elwend, and gave phonetic values to 120 characters. He was, however, still under the belief that they represented letters instead of syllables, and was consequently obliged to admit the existence of 'homophones.' The fact that they really represented syllables,—*ba*, *bi*, *be*, *bu*, &c.—was discovered by Dr. Hincks immediately afterwards (1847 and 1850). Hincks also discovered the name of Nebuchadrezzar in the Babylonian inscriptions, and by the further discovery that an inscription brought from Babylon by Sir Robert Ker-Porter, which was written in the complicated characters of early Babylonia, was a duplicate of one in the ' Neo-Babylonian ' characters of the Achaemenian era, he made it possible to read the oldest forms of Babylonian script. From this time forward the work of decipherment went on apace. The Semitic character of the Assyro-Babylonian language, which had been guessed at by Löwenstern, was now put beyond question, and the well-known laws of Semitic grammar came to the help of the student in reading the text. In 1851 Rawlinson published the Babylonian text of the Behistun inscription, and in his commentary upon it announced to a wondering and incredulous world the existence in Assyrian of 'polyphones.' If the method of decipherment were right, it was necessary to assume that the same character could have more than one phonetic value. The cause of this extraordinary fact—which, however, is paralleled in Old Egyptian as well as in Japanese— was soon made clear by Oppert, Hincks, and Rawlinson himself. The Assyrian syllabary, which had originally

C

been a collection of pictorial hieroglyphs, was not the invention of the Semitic Babylonians, but of an earlier people who spoke an agglutinative language, and to whom the name of Accadians or Sumerians was given. When the script was adopted by the Semites, the Sumerian words denoting the objects or ideas for which the characters stood became phonetic values; thus *du* 'to go' and *gub* 'to stand' became the phonetic values of the character which had originally been a picture of a human leg.

The interpretation of the Assyrian and Babylonian texts now advanced rapidly, in spite of the smallness of the body of students, and the incredulity of Orientalists, especially in Germany. In 1847 Rawlinson was able to give a fairly complete account of the several varieties of cuneiform writing, and in 1850 he published a translation of the long inscription of Shalmaneser II on the Black Obelisk of Nimrûd. The translation is on the whole marvellously correct, and proves conclusively the soundness of the method on which it was based. The proper names, however, were still but imperfectly read, and it was not till Hincks discovered the names of Jehu and Omri in the inscription (in 1851) that the age of it could be fixed. Shortly afterwards Hincks deciphered the

names of Hezekiah and Jerusalem in the texts of
Sennacherib, as well as the name of Sennacherib
himself, and thus showed that Longpérier had been
right in his conjecture that the king of the Khorsabad
monuments was Sargon. The foundation of Assyrian
grammar was next laid by Hincks in 1855 in a series
of remarkable articles on the Assyrian verb, to which
the progress of discovery has since added little that is
important. A complete and systematic grammar itself
was first written by Dr. Oppert in 1860, and eight
years afterwards M. Ménant analyzed his results and
tested their correctness.

The Decipherment tested.—Orientalists, however, still looked askance at the new science which
threatened to dwarf the older Semitic learning. The
Council of the Royal Asiatic Society, accordingly, determined to subject it to a conclusive test. Copies of the
annals of Tiglath-pileser I, which had been found at
Kalah Sherghat, were sent to Rawlinson, Hincks,
Fox Talbot, and Oppert ; they were asked to translate
them independently of one another, and send the
translations under seal by a given date to the Secretary
of the Society. When the translations were opened
they were found to be in substantial agreement. This

was in 1857, a year which we may therefore regard as closing the first epoch of decipherment.

Sumerian.—The decipherment of the Assyrian texts brought with it the decipherment of the Sumerian texts. The library of Nineveh was stocked with tablets intended to facilitate the study of the old language of Chaldaea. Among them are grammars, vocabularies, and reading-books, as well as interlinear or parallel translations of Sumerian texts in the Semitic language of Babylon and Assyria. Oppert in his *Expédition scientifique en Mésopotamie* led the way to the use of them in 1859, and the outlines of Sumerian grammar were first sketched by Sayce in 1870, followed by Lenormant in 1873. Since then the labours of Lenormant, Haupt (who demonstrated the existence of two Accado-Sumerian dialects), Hommel, Amiaud, Ball and others, have given us an extensive knowledge of the primitive language of Babylonia.

Vannic.—Northward of Assyria, in Ararat, the modern Armenia, the cuneiform script of Nineveh had been borrowed in the ninth century B. C. As the characters of the script continued to preserve their Assyrian values there was no difficulty in transliterating them, and as early as 1852 Hincks read the names of the kings they had been employed to write, and even used them in determining the values of the characters found at Nineveh. The majority of the inscriptions, which had been copied by Schulz at the cost of his life in 1829, and published in France in 1840, were met with in the neighbourhood of Van; hence the term 'Vannic' which is usually applied to them. The language in which they are written was however utterly unknown, and bore no obvious relationship to any with which we are acquainted ; consequently though the texts could be transliterated they could not be translated. More than one attempt was made to decipher them, but to no purpose, until 1882 when Guyard pointed out that the formula with which many of them end corresponds with the imprecation often attached to the Assyrian inscriptions, and Sayce, following up this clue, with the help of the ideographs borrowed from Assyria, finally succeeded in solving the problem. A bilingual text (Assyrian and Vannic), recently discovered by M. de Morgan in the pass of Kelishin in Kurdistan, has verified the correctness of his results, which have been further modified or extended by D. H. Müller, Belck, and Lehmann.

Other Languages.—Yet two more languages

written in the cuneiform syllabary have lately been revealed by the cuneiform tablets found at Tel el-Amarna in Upper Egypt. One was the language of Mitanni, the Aram-Naharaim of the Old Testament, in which there is a long letter from the king of Mitanni to the Egyptian Pharaoh. The other language, which is quite distinct from that of Mitanni, was spoken at Arzawa in northern Syria. Both languages are still undeciphered [1].

The origin of the Cuneiform Syllabary.—As we have seen, the pictorial origin of the cuneiform characters was perceived in the early days of Assyrian decipherment, as well as the cause of their polyphony. Their wedge-like forms were due to the use of clay as a writing material. The impression made by the stylus upon it resembled a wedge; curved lines became angles, and after a time the original picture passed into a conventional form. In the course of centuries the characters grew more and more simplified by the omission of unnecessary wedges, the

---

[1] For the language of Mitanni, called that of Su(ri) in the Assyrian lexical lists, see Jensen, Brünnow, and myself in the *Zeitschrift für Assyriologie*, v. 2, 3 (Aug. 1890), and for that of Arzawa see my letter to the *Academy*, Aug. 20, 1892, pp. 154, 155.

least complicated being those of the official hand of Assyria, and the later Babylonian or Persepolitan script. It must not be supposed, however, that when the system of writing ceased to be pictorial it was already complete. Down to a comparatively late period new characters were invented or old characters combined in a new way, while new phonetic and ideographic values were assigned to the characters which already existed. Though the syllabary is essentially of Sumerian origin there is much in it which is traceable to a Semitic source. Many of the values given to the characters as well as many of their ideographic meanings are Semitic. Moreover the Sumerians and Semites lived in contact with one another long after the adoption of Sumerian culture by the Semitic nomads; consequently not only did the Semites borrow Sumerian words, the Sumerians borrowed Semitic words, more especially in the northern part of the country. The early date at which some of these were borrowed is shown by their having undergone the phonetic changes which distinguished the northern Accado-Sumerian dialect from the southern. False etymologizing also has given rise to new values just as it has given rise to new spellings in English. The Semitic scribes of a later day were as fond of deriving Semitic words from Sumerian as our own etymologists used to be of deriving Teutonic words from Latin, Greek, or Hebrew. Thus the purely Semitic *sabattu* 'Sabbath,' from *sabâtu* 'to rest,' is derived from the two Sumerian words *sa* 'heart' and *bat* 'to complete,' and interpreted to mean 'a day of rest for the heart.'

Simplification of the Syllabary.—The script used at Susa before the overthrow of the kingdom of Elam was the same as the archaic script of Babylonia. But the Amardian syllabary was a selected one. Not only were the forms of the characters simplified, a comparatively small number of them was employed to each of which one value only was assigned. In the Vannic texts also polyphony was similarly avoided. Characters expressing open syllables like *ba* and *ab* were chosen, to which a few more denoting closed syllables and ideographs were added ; but in no case was a character allowed to possess more than one value. Large use was further made of the vowels, the syllable *ba*, for example, being written *ba-a*, so that the syllabary tended to become an alphabet. This step was taken in Old Persian, where the forms of the letters were often so simplified as to lose all resemblance to their primitive forms. Apart from its alphabet of thirty-six letters Old Persian retained only one syllabic character (*tr*) and a few ideographs.

The pictorial origin of the syllabary has proved of important assistance in reading the texts. Certain of the ideographs were used as 'determinatives' for indicating the generic character of the word to which they are prefixed or affixed. Thus there is a determinative to denote that the word which follows is the name of a 'city,' and another which shows that the preceding word is a plural. In this way a glance at an Assyrian, an Amardian, or a Vannic text will enable us at once to distinguish the names of men, women, towns, countries, animals, trees, metals, stones, and the like. It is a help which we look for in vain in Phoenician or Hebrew inscriptions.

CHAPTER III

Different States in Babylonia. — More than one kingdom originally existed in Babylonia. Not only were there separate kingdoms in Accad and Sumer, or northern and southern Chaldaea, many of the great cities also once formed separate states. The excavations at Tello, for instance, have revealed the existence of a dynasty which had its seat there, and the ancestral kingdom of Sargon of Accad does not seem to have extended beyond the territory of its chief city. The smaller states were, however, absorbed by the larger ones, and a time came when the whole of Babylonia was united into a single monarchy, whose ruler assumed the imperial title of ' king of Sumer and Accad.' As in Egypt, therefore, a recollection of the original dual character of the kingdom was preserved in the title of its kings.

It is probable that the various states of Babylonia were more than once brought into temporary union before the final unification of the monarchy took place. Sargon of Accad, for instance, seems to have claimed supremacy over the rest of Chaldaea, and the dynasties which subsequently arose at Ur and other places adopted the imperial title, although the country was not finally united under a single head until the reign of Khammurabi. It was to this early period that the maritime trade and civilizing influence of Eridu chiefly belongs.

The first Empire.—Sargon of Accad founded the earliest Semitic empire of which we know. According to Nabonidos he lived more than 3,200 years before the time of the last Babylonian king, that is to say about 3800 B.C. His father, Itti-Bel, had no royal title, and legend gathered around his birth. His uncle, it was said, ruled in the mountains, and his mother concealed her child in an ark of rushes, daubed with pitch, which she entrusted to the waters of the Euphrates. Here he was found by a peasant, who brought him up as his own son. But the goddess Istar loved the peasant lad, and the time at last came when he was able to declare his true character and ascend the throne of his fathers.

A copy has been preserved of the historical annals of Sargon and his son Naram-Sin, which must have been compiled in the reign of the latter, as they break off in the middle of it. We learn from them that Sargon not only established his rule over Babylonia and the adjoining districts, he also defeated the Elamites, and made four expeditions into Syria, 'the land of the Amorites.' The last of these expeditions occupied three years, and ended with the erection of images of the Chaldaean king on the shores of the Mediterranean, and with the conquest of the countries ' of the sea of the setting sun,' which he united ' into a single empire.' His last campaign was against the Aram-Naharaim of Scripture in north-western Mesopotamia. Babylon is already mentioned as one of his seats of power; his capital, however, was at Agade or Accad, where on one occasion he was unsuccessfully besieged by his revolted subjects. Here, too, he founded a famous library, for which the standard work on astronomy and astrology was compiled in seventy-two books. A translation of it into Greek was made in later days by the Chaldaean historian Bêrôssos.

Sargon's son and successor Naram-Sin continued his father's victorious career, and Palestine being already secured behind him, marched into the land of

Magan, by which name Midian and the Sinaitic peninsula were known, and captured its king. A record of the conquest was engraved on an alabaster vase discovered by the French Expedition to Babylonia, but unfortunately lost in the Tigris. Naram-Sin, like one or two other Babylonian monarchs of the same early epoch, received divine honours.

The monuments of Tello.—The oldest monuments found at Tello in southern Chaldaea belong to the age of Sargon and Naram-Sin. But whereas the court of Sargon was Semitic, that of the kings of Tello was Sumerian. At a later date Tello lost its independence, and its rulers became merely *patesis* or high-priests. One of these was Gudea, whose statue may be seen in the Louvre. In his time building-materials were brought to Chaldaea from all parts of Western Asia ; thus cedar beams were imported from Mount Amanus, and diorite from the land of Magan. It was out of this diorite that the statues were cut. Another of the *patesis* of Tello was the vassal of Dungi, king of Ur, whose father had built or restored the great temple of the Moon-god in that city, and had claimed sovereignty over the whole of Babylonia.

Chronology.—These early sovereigns are known
to us by the bricks and other objects which they have
left behind, but we cannot arrange them in a chronological order. Chronology begins with what is called
by the native historians 'the dynasty of Babylon.'
From this time forward the tablets have preserved the
names of the Babylonian kings divided into dynasties,
together with the length of each reign as well as of each
dynasty. The sixth king of the dynasty of Babylon was
Khammurabi, who reigned fifty-five years (B. C. 2356–
2301)[1], and whose reign marks an epoch in Babylonian
history.

The United Monarchy. — When Khammurabi
ascended the throne, Babylonia was either wholly or
in part under Elamite suzerainty. That portion of it
of which Larsa was the capital was governed by Eri-
Aku (probably the Arioch of Genesis), who was a son
of the Elamite prince Kudur-Mabug. Kudur-Mabug
was not himself king, but as he has the title of 'father
of the land of the Amorites' he must have held rule

[1] The date partly depends upon the number of years assigned
to the dynasty to which Nabonassar belonged, which unfortunately is not stated by the native historians. Consequently,
other Assyriologists make it, sometimes a little higher, sometimes
a little lower. For the justification of my date see the *Records
of the Past*, New Series, pp. viii–xi.

in Syria. Khammurabi succeeded in overthrowing Eri-Aku and his Elamite allies and in making himself sole king of Babylonia. Babylon, his capital, thus became, and remained, the capital of the united kingdom. It was soon the scene of a great literary revival. The older literature of the country was re-edited, new authors arose, and the court of Khammurabi revived the literary glories of that of Sargon. As his great-grandson still calls himself 'king of the land of the Amorites' we may infer that the conquests in Syria were not lost.

The rise of Assyria.—The dynasty of Khammurabi was followed by one which came from Tello, whose kings bear Sumerian names. Then Babylonia was conquered by Kassite princes who ruled over it for 576 years and nine months (B. C. 1806–1229). While the Kassite dynasty was reigning, a new kingdom arose in the north, that of Assyria. The high-priests of the city of Assur became kings, the first of whom seems to have been Bel-Kapkapu. The kingdom rapidly grew in power, and although Babylonia exacted tribute from it, its kings began to ally themselves by marriage with the rulers of the southern monarchy. In the fifteenth century B. C. Assur-

yuballidh of Assyria, like his contemporary Burna-
buryas of Babylonia, sent letters and presents to the
Egyptian Pharaoh and begged in return for Egyptian
gold, and a century later the city of Calah was built
(or restored) by Shalmaneser I. His son Tiglath-Uras
in the sixth year of his reign marched against Babylonia, captured Babylon and governed it for seven
years. He was then driven out of the country and
subsequently murdered by his own son. The Kassite
dynasty, however, did not last long after the Assyrian
invasion. The Assyrian king had entered Babylon in
B. C. 1291, and in B. C. 1229 the dynasty came to
an end.

Babylon a sacred city.—From this time forward
for many centuries Assyria, and not Babylonia, occu-
pies the chief place in the history of western Asia. It
needed a Nebuchadrezzar to make Babylonia once
more a conquering power. But Babylon itself remained the sacred city of the cultured nations of
Asia. Its old *prestige* and hallowed associations
clung to it, and it became what Rome was to
mediaeval Europe. An Assyrian king, however
powerful he might be, could not claim the imperial
title until he had 'taken the hands of Bel' and

thereby been adopted as a son by the god of Babylon. Indeed it was only in this way that usurpers like Tiglath-pileser III and Sargon obtained any recognition of their legitimate right to the throne. The sanction of religion remained with Babylon, though the sword had passed to Assyria.

Tiglath-pileser I.—One of the most famous of the early Assyrian conquerors was Tiglath-pileser I (B. C. 1100). He carried his arms in all directions. Eastward he chastised the Kurds, northward he penetrated into the mountains of Armenia and engraved his image at the sources of the Tigris; and in the west he overthrew the Moschians, the Meshech of the Bible, ravaging the land of Komagênê, laying Malatiyeh under tribute, threatening the Hittites in their stronghold at Carchemish, and making his way to the shores of the Mediterranean. Here he sailed over the sea in a ship of Arvad, and received presents from the terrified Pharaoh of Egypt which comprised a crocodile and a hippopotamus. Southward he invaded Babylonia, and though repulsed in his first attack he avenged himself by subsequently overrunning the country and capturing Babylon. He was also mighty in the hunting-field as well as in war,

D

and in the neighbourhood of Harran boasts of
having slain the wild elephants which then existed
there. His own capital Assur he adorned with the
spoils of his victories and restored its temples.

The First Assyrian Empire.—We have to pass
over an interval of two centuries before we find
another Assyrian monarch who emulated the distant
campaigns of Tiglath-pileser. Assur-natsir-pal (B. C.
883–858) was the first of a line of conquerors who
may be regarded as the founders of the first Assyrian
empire. From henceforth, too, Assyrian chronology
is accurately fixed. The Assyrians counted time by
means of certain officers called *limmi*, who were
changed from year to year. The name of a particular
limmu consequently indicated the year during which
he had held office. Lists of the *limmi* have been
preserved which begin with the reign of Assur-natsir-
pal's father and carry us down to that of Assur-bani-
pal. As the annals not only of Tiglath-pileser I, but
also of an older king, the father of Shalmaneser I,
are dated in the years of office of certain *limmi* it is
clear that the institution went back to an early period,
and that lists of the older *limmi* may yet be recovered,
carrying us, it may be, to the very foundation of the
Assyrian kingdom.

Calah, instead of Assur, had become the royal residence, and from Calah accordingly the Assyrian armies marched forth year after year to conquer and spoil. The fastnesses of the Kurdish mountains were explored, and the Kurdish tribes compelled to pay tribute to the Assyrian king. The cities of Armenia south of Lake Van were ravaged in repeated campaigns, one effect of which seems to have been the introduction of Assyrian culture and writing, and the rise of the Vannic monarchy. The merchant princes of Carchemish bought off the Assyrian attack with rich gifts, but the states on either bank of the Euphrates were overrun, and Assur-natsir-pal made his way across Amanus to the Gulf of Antioch, and across Lebanon to the Mediterranean. Here he received the tribute of the Phoenician cities, among them being Tyre and Sidon. In imitation of Tiglath-pileser I he hunted in northern Mesopotamia, but the elephant had disappeared from the region, and he had to content himself with the wild bull.

Assur-natsir-pal was succeeded by his son Shalmaneser II, whose reign ended in B. C. 823. His long reign was a series of military campaigns. Countries previously untrodden by Assyrian feet were subdued or ravaged with fire and sword. Assyrian

D 2

armies made their way through the passes of Kurdistan as far as Lake Urumiyeh and the land of the Minni. The newly-founded kingdom of Ararat was shaken, the Tibareni (called Tubal in Scripture) paid tribute, and Tarsus in Cilicia was compelled to open its gates. The passage of the Euphrates was secured by the capture of the Hittite fortress of Pethor at the junction of the Euphrates and the Sajur, and the whole weight of the Assyrian power was hurled against Syria. The Phoenician cities made their peace with the invader by offering gifts ; so too did Jehu (Yahua) of Samaria, whose ambassadors are represented on the Black Obelisk. Hamath and Damascus, more especially the latter, had to bear the brunt of the Assyrian attack. In B. C. 853, thirteen years before the embassy of Jehu, Israel and Assyria had already met in the battle-field. A league had been formed by Hamath, Arvad, Ammon, and other states under the leadership of Hadadezer of Damascus—the Ben-hadad of the Old Testament—to resist the Assyrians, and one of the most important of the allies was 'Ahab of Israel,' who brought into the field 2,000 chariots and 10,000 men. But the confederacy was shattered at the battle of Qarqar, though Shalmaneser's own losses were too serious to allow him to follow up the attack. In B. C. 847 Hadadezer and his allies were again defeated, but without any result on the Assyrian side. Seven years later Hazael appears in the place of Hadadezer. Shalmaneser drove him from his camp into Damascus, where he 'shut him up,' taking from him 1,121 chariots and devastating the country as far as the Hauran. It was on this occasion that Jehu offered homage to the conqueror. Shalmaneser had already overrun Babylonia and sacrificed to the gods in Babylon, Borsippa, and Cutha. The Babylonian king was put to death, and the Assyrian troops penetrated into the salt-marshes of the Kaldâ in the extreme south. For a time, therefore, the larger part of western Asia lay at the feet of 'the great king.'

A time came, however, when Shalmaneser could no longer lead his armies in person, but had to entrust them to the Tartan or commander-in-chief. His own son Assur-dain-pal rebelled against him, and led the chief cities of his kingdom, including Nineveh and Assur, into revolt (B. C. 827). The revolt lasted for more than six years, and during its continuance the old king was succeeded by his son Samsi-Rimmon who eventually suppressed the insurrection. Assur-dain-pal seems to have been the original Sardanapallos of the Greeks. The campaigns of Samsi-Rimmon were principally directed against the Kurds and Medes, but towards the end of his reign he invaded Babylonia and defeated its king, Merodach-balásu-iqbi, the Greek Belesys. His successor Rimmon-nirari III (B. C. 810–781) claims to have overcome Media and Kurdistan, Tyre, Sidon, Samaria, and Palastu, 'the land of the Philistines,' under which title the Jews would be included. But his chief exploit was the conquest of Damascus, whose king Marih opened its gates to him and became an Assyrian vassal.

The older Assyrian dynasty, however, was fast coming to an end. In B. C. 753 its last representative, Assur-nirari, mounted the throne. Insurrection had already broken out at the beginning of his predecessor's reign, and pestilence had been added to insurrection. The old capital Assur had led the revolt, a solar eclipse on June 15, B. C. 763 coinciding with its outbreak. The northern provinces had followed the lead of Assur, and though the revolt was crushed for a while, the flame of discontent still smouldered beneath the surface. The greater part of Assur-nirari's short reign was passed in inaction, but in B. C. 746 Calah rebelled, and on the

13th of Iyyar in the following year Pulu or Pul, who took the name of Tiglath-pileser III, after that of the great conqueror of the older dynasty, was proclaimed king. With him begins the history of the second Assyrian empire.

The Second Assyrian Empire.—With the second Assyrian empire a new political idea entered the world. Most of the campaigns made by the earlier Assyrian kings were mere raids, the object of which was booty and captives. It is true that in some cases cities and districts were annexed to the Assyrian kingdom and Assyrian colonists were planted in distant localities. But this was the exception, not the rule. The conquests made in one year by the Assyrian armies had to be made over again in the next. The campaigns of Tiglath-pileser III and his successors had a different object in view. They aimed at bringing the whole civilized world under the rule of ' the great king.' A great political organization was to be built up, which should bring the wealth of Western Asia into the imperial treasury of Nineveh and divert the trade of Phoenicia and Babylon into Assyrian hands. Trade interests had much to do with the wars of the New Empire.

Accordingly, while the frontiers of the kingdom were secured from the wild tribes on the east and north, expedition after expedition was sent westward and southward which pushed steadily forward the Assyrian domination. Satraps and colonists followed in the wake of the generals; and the amount of annual tribute to be paid by each province was defined and rigorously exacted from its governor. The latter was appointed by the king, and held his office at the royal pleasure. At his side were military officers, and under him a body of officials who were responsible to the governor as he was to the king.

The New Empire was thus governed by a vast bureaucracy, at the head of which stood the king. But the bureaucracy was military as well as civil, and the military and civil elements formed a check one upon the other. The military element was, however, predominant, the result of the fact that the empire itself was based on conquest.

The army was carefully trained, well disciplined, and well armed. It thus soon became an irresistible weapon in the hands of a competent master. Before Tiglath-pileser's reign was half over there was no force in western Asia which was capable of resisting it in open fight.

Tiglath-pileser reigned eighteen years (B.C. 745–727), and his organizing abilities proved to be as great as his military skill. An invasion of Babylonia first tested the strength of his army, and resulted in the subjection of the Aramaean tribes in that country to Assyrian rule. Then followed an expedition into Kurdistan. The Medes were massacred, and the Assyrian army pushed its way far eastward to Bikni, 'the mountain of the rising sun.' Next Tiglath-pileser turned to the north-west. Here he was met by a powerful confederacy, at the head of which was the king of Ararat. But the forces of the northern nations were cut to pieces in Komagene, and Arpad, which had become the centre of a hostile Syrian league, was captured after a siege of three years. The league had included Hamath and Azariah of Judah, and Hamath was consequently annexed to the Assyrian empire. The princes of the West hastened to offer homage to the conqueror, among them being Rezon of Damascus and Menahem of Samaria (B.C. 738). Tiglath-pileser was now free to march against Ararat, which had extended its power at the expense of Assyria in the later days of the old dynasty. The country was ravaged up to the gates of its capital, and the Vannic kingdom received a blow from which it never recovered. The Assyrian army next turned eastward to the southern shores of the Caspian, and made its way through Medic and other districts which neither before nor since were trodden by Assyrian feet. The exploit struck terror into the Kurdish tribes, and secured the Assyrian lowlands from their attack.

Meanwhile Ahaz of Judah had been threatened by Rezon of Damascus and Pekah of Israel, and he now appealed to the Assyrian king for help. Tiglath-pileser, nothing loth, marched against the assailants. Rezon was blockaded in his capital, while Samaria, Ammon, Moab, and Philistia were overrun (B.C. 734). Two years later (B.C. 732), Damascus was taken and sacked, Rezon put to death and his kingdom placed under an Assyrian prefect. Pekah, too, had been murdered, and Tiglath-pileser had appointed Hosea king in his place. About the same time Tyre was compelled to purchase peace by the payment of 150 talents.

With his empire consolidated in the west, and the road to the Mediterranean open to Assyrian trade, Tiglath-pileser was now free to legitimize his right to the throne by occupying Babylon and there becoming the adopted son of Bel. It was in B.C. 731 that the

Babylonian campaign began; in B. C. 729 Tiglath-pileser, under his original name of Pul, 'took the hands of Bel,' and two years later, in the month of December, he died. He had introduced into history the idea of imperial centralization.

On his death the crown was seized by Ululâ, who took the name of Shalmaneser IV. His reign lasted only five years, and when he died (December, B. C. 722) he was pressing the siege of Samaria. The capture of the city and its annexation to Assyria were the work of Sargon. The upper and military classes, amounting in all to 27,280 persons, were carried into captivity; but only fifty chariots were found in the city.

Sargon was a usurper like his two predecessors, but, more fortunate than they, he succeeded in founding a dynasty. He was one of the best generals that Assyria ever produced, and under him the extension and organization of the empire went on apace. The death of Shalmaneser, however, had been the signal for revolt in Babylonia as well as in the west. Merodach-baladan, a Chaldaean from the sea-marshes, had seized Babylon in conjunction with the Elamites, and there reigned as legitimate monarch for twelve years. One of the first tasks of Sargon was to drive the Elamite forces from the Assyrian frontier. Ha-

math moreover rose in insurrection; but this too
was speedily crushed. So also was a league between
the Philistines and the Egyptians; the battle of
Raphia decided, once for all, the question of Assyrian
supremacy in Palestine.

Sargon now had to face a more formidable coali-
tion, that of the northern nations under Ursa of
Ararat. The struggle lasted for six years and ended
with the complete victory of the Assyrians. Carchemish, the Hittite stronghold on the Euphrates,
fell in B.C. 717, leaving the road clear to the west
and thus uniting Assyria with its rising empire on
the shores of the Mediterranean. In the following
year the Minni (to the east of Ararat) were overthrown, and two years later Ursa and his allies were
utterly defeated. The fortress of Muzazir near Lake
Urumiyeh was captured, thus extending the Assyrian
frontier far to the east, and Ursa, in despair, com-
mitted suicide. Media was completely subdued in
B.C. 713, and Ellip, where Ekbatana afterwards stood,
became the vassal of Nineveh. In B.C. 711 a league
was formed between Merodach-baladan and the
nations of southern Syria to resist the common foe,
and to this league Egypt promised assistance. But
before the confederates were ready to act, Sargon had

fallen upon them separately. Ashdod, the centre of the Palestinian confederacy, was besieged and taken (Isaiah xxi), and its ruler, a certain 'Greek,' who had been raised to power by the anti-Assyrian party, fled in vain for refuge to the Arabian desert, while Judah, Edom, and Moab were compelled to pay tribute. In B. C. 709 Merodach-baladan was driven out of Babylonia into his ancestral kingdom of Bit-Yagna. Sargon entered Babylon and there 'took the hands of Bel.' Henceforward he ruled by divine right as well as by the right of the sword.

It was by the sword, however, that he perished, being murdered by a soldier in B. C. 705. His son Sennacherib succeeded to the crown on the 12th of Ab (July). Sennacherib was a different man from his father; boastfulness and vanity took the place of military skill; perhaps also of courage. There seems to have been some resemblance between his character and that of Xerxes.

Babylonia was the new king's first object of attack. Merodach-baladan, who had re-entered Babylon on the news of Sargon's death, was driven back to the marshes, and Bel-ibni, an Assyrian vassal, appointed king in his place. The next campaign was against the Kassi or Kossaeans, some of whom were forced

to descend from their mountain fastnesses and placed
under an Assyrian governor.   From the Kossaean
mountains the Assyrian army marched into Ellip
which was wasted with fire and sword.   Then, in
B. C. 701, came the campaign against Palestine where
Hezekiah of Judah, in reliance upon Egypt, had
revolted from his Assyrian lord.   Elulaeus of Sidon
fled to Cyprus, and Phoenicia, Ammon, Moab, and
Edom submitted to the Assyrians.   Sennacherib
thereupon proceeded against the Philistines.   A new
king was set over Ashkelon, and Hezekiah was compelled to restore to Ekron its former prince whom he
had imprisoned in Jerusalem on account of his faith-
fulness to Assyria.   The priests and nobles of Ekron
who had abetted Hezekiah were impaled on stakes.

Tirhakah, the Ethiopian king of Egypt, and the
king of Melukh (the Arabian desert), who had come
to the assistance of the Jewish prince, were defeated
at Eltekeh, and Hezekiah vainly endeavoured to buy
off the vengeance of his offended suzerain by rich and
numerous presents, including 30 talents of gold and
800 talents of silver.   The surrender of Jerusalem
alone would content Sennacherib, who accordingly
devastated Judah, destroying its cities and carrying
into captivity 200,150 of its inhabitants.   Jerusalem

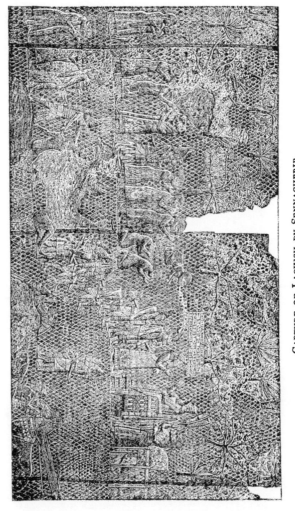

CAPTURE OF LACHISH BY SENNACHERIB.

itself was blockaded, Hezekiah being shut up in it 'like a bird in a cage.' Then, however, came the catastrophe which obliged Sennacherib to retire without punishing his rebellious vassal, and of which, of course, nothing is said in the inscriptions. But there is no further record of a campaign in the West. In the following year Sennacherib was in Babylonia, where he drove Merodach-baladan out of the marshes and obliged the Chaldaean prince and his subjects to fly in ships across the Persian Gulf to the opposite coast of Elam. Assur-nadin-suma, the son of Sennacherib, was now made king of Babylon. Six years later he was carried off to Elam and a new king, Nergal-yusezib, appointed in his place by the Elamite monarch. This was in return for an unprovoked assault made by Sennacherib on the Chaldaean colony in Elam, to which he had crossed in boats made by Tyrian workmen, and whose inhabitants he sent captive to Assyria.

For a time Elam was all-powerful in Babylonia, though Nergal-yusezib had been defeated and captured in battle by the Assyrians. But in b.c. 691 Sennacherib descended with the full might of Assyria upon the country. The Babylonians had sent the treasures of the temple of Bel to the Elamite monarch, begging his help. The Babylonian and Elamite forces met

E

the army of Assyria at Khalule, and a hard-fought battle was the result. The slaughter was great on both sides, and Sennacherib claims a complete victory, though the Babylonian Chronicle—a cuneiform document compiled from a Babylonian point of view—implies that such was not altogether the case. At all events about two years were needed for the subjugation of Babylonia. In B.C. 689 Babylon was taken, its houses and temples destroyed, the images of its gods broken in pieces, and the ruins of the city thrown into the Arakhtu, the canal of Babylon. For some years Babylon lay desolate, and as there was no longer a temple or image of Bel to legitimize the rule of the Assyrian conqueror, Babylonia remained 'without kings.'

On the 20th day of Tebet or December, B.C. 681, Sennacherib was murdered by two of his sons who seem to have been jealous of their brother Esar-haddon. Esar-haddon had been given the new name of Assur-etil-mukin-abla ('Assur the hero is the establisher of my son'), perhaps because he had been destined for the throne, and at the time of his father's murder he was commanding the Assyrian army in a war against Ararat. For forty-two days the conspirators held the capital; then they were compelled to fly to Erimenas of Ararat and seek his help against their brother. The decisive battle was fought on the 12th of Iyyar (April) near Malatiyeh in Kappadokia ; the veterans of Assyria won the day, and at the close of it saluted Esar-haddon as king. He returned to Nineveh and on the 8th of Sivan (May) formally ascended the throne.

Esar-haddon was great in counsel as well as in war, and knew how to conciliate as well as how to conquer. At the outset of his reign he restored Babylon, rebuilt its temples, brought back its gods and people, and made it one of his royal residences. For twelve years he was king alike of Babylonia and Assyria.

A revolt of Sidon, which was easily put down, next occupied his attention. Then came a more formidable event. The Gimirrâ, called Gomer in Genesis, Kimmerians by the Greeks, suddenly appeared out of the north and menaced the civilized world. Esar-haddon met them on the frontier of his empire, defeated their chieftain, the 'Manda' or nomad Teuspa, and drove his hordes westward into Asia Minor. It now became necessary to secure the Assyrian frontier on the south. The Assyrian king accordingly marched into the very heart of Arabia, through burning and waterless deserts, and struck terror into the Arabian tribes.

The march must have been one of the most remarkable ever made.

Esar-haddon was at last free to complete the policy of Tiglath-pileser III by conquering the ancient kingdom of Egypt. Palestine gave no more trouble; Manasseh of Judah was already an obedient vassal of the Assyrian king. In B.C. 674 'the Assyrians marched into Egypt.' But two more campaigns were needed for its subjection. In B.C. 670 Esar-haddon drove the Egyptian forces before him in fifteen days (from the 3rd to the 18th of Tammuz or June) all the way from the frontier to Memphis, thrice defeating them with heavy loss and wounding Tirhakah their king. Three days later Memphis fell, and Tirhakah fled to Ethiopia, leaving Egypt to the conqueror. Egypt revolted two years afterwards (B.C. 668), and while on the march to reduce it Esar-haddon fell ill, and died on the 10th of Marchesvan or October. Assur-banipal, who had already been named as his successor, became king of Assyria, his brother Saul-suma-yukin taking Babylonia as his share. The king of Babylonia, however, was required to admit the supremacy of the Assyrian monarch.

The Egyptian revolt was quickly suppressed and the country was again divided into twenty satrapies, each satrapy being placed under a native prince. But the arrangement answered badly. The satraps quarrelled with one another, intrigued with Tirhakah, and rebelled against Assur-bani-pal. Time after time Assyrian armies had to be sent to reconquer the land. Once Necho, the satrap of Sais, was brought in chains to Nineveh, there, however, to be pardoned and restored to his city. Twice Thebes was captured, once after it had been made for a time the seat of Tirhakah's government, a second time after the defeat of Urdaman (Rud-Amon), the step-son and successor of Tirhakah. On this occasion the city was utterly destroyed. Its temples and palaces were overthrown, its statues mutilated, and an immense spoil carried away to Nineveh. Among the spoil were two obelisks, over seventy tons in weight. The destruction of Thebes is alluded to by the prophet Nahum (iii. 8).

Assur-bani-pal, the Sardanapallos of the Greeks, was the 'Grand Monarque' of Assyria, and a generous patron of literature and learning. But he lacked the warlike instincts of his fathers, and preferred to remain at home while his generals fought in the field. His long wars drained the country of its fighting-men and prepared the way for its downfall. They were waged mainly with Elam, the only civilized country of

Western Asia which still preserved its independence, and lasted for several years. At last, however, Elam fell; its capital Shushan was sacked and burned, and a desolated country was added to the Assyrian dominions.

The fame of Assur-bani-pal spread far and wide. Ambassadors came to his court from Ararat, as well as from Gyges of Lydia. At first no interpreter could be found for the latter. Gyges wanted help against the Kimmerians, which, however, 'the great king' does not seem to have afforded. The tribute of Gyges was accordingly withdrawn after a time, and he took part in the great rebellion which now shook the Assyrian empire to its foundations.

Saul-suma-yukin put himself at its head, and proclaimed the independence of Babylonia. Psammetikhos, the son of Necho of Sais, imitated his example in Egypt, and with the assistance of Gyges put down the rival satraps, shook off the Assyrian yoke and founded the Twenty-sixth dynasty. Saul-suma-yukin was less fortunate. After a desperate struggle he was captured and put to death by his brother, and Babylonia was once more reduced to servitude. Punishment was also taken upon the tribes of northern Arabia who had joined the rebels.

But the empire was terribly weakened. Egypt was lost to it for ever, and though Elam was added instead, it proved to be a barren possession. When Tuktamme the ' Manda' appeared upon the scene he was resisted with difficulty. The empire was tottering to its fall.

Of its closing days we know but little from the monuments. Among the successors of Assur-bani-pal were Assur-etil-ilani-yukin (who still claimed rule in Babylonia), and Sin-sar-iskun. The latter has sometimes been identified with Sarakos, said by the Greek writer Abydênos to have been the last king of Assyria [1]. At all events the fall and destruction of Nineveh may be placed in B.C. 606.

The Babylonian Empire.—On its ruins rose the Babylonian empire of Nebuchadrezzar, the son of Nabopolassar. The battle of Carchemish placed him in possession of Syria, which the Egyptians had occupied after the fall of Nineveh. The battle was scarcely over when Nebuchadrezzar was recalled to Babylon by the death of his father (B.C. 605). Unlike the Assyrian kings, he cared but little about recording his

---

[1] A contract-tablet exists dated at Sippara in the second year of Sin-sar-iskun, which shows that the rule of the king was acknowledged in Babylonia.

successes in war.   His inscriptions are occupied with
the account of his building operations, of his gifts to
the gods, and of his devotion to Bel Merodach.   Under
him Babylon became one of the most splendid cities
in the world.   Its palaces, its temples, its hanging
gardens and its walls were alike on a vast and magnifi-
cent scale.   The temples were roofed with cedar of
Lebanon, overlaid with gold and silver, and the ram-
parts of the royal house were finished in fifteen days.
The suburb of Borsippa was included within the forti-
fications of the city, which were so strong as to be
practicably impregnable.   At the same time the
other cities of Babylonia were not forgotten, and
their temples were enlarged and beautified.

   In B.C. 568 Nebuchadrezzar marched into Egypt,
defeated the Pharaoh Amasis and occupied a part at
least of the Delta.   'Phut of the Ionians' is mentioned in connexion with this campaign.   It is the
only military expedition mentioned in the texts we
possess ; even the monuments of Nebuchadrezzar
found in Syria (at the mouth of the Nahr el-Kelb near
Beyrout and in the Wadi Brissa near the ancient
Riblah) are silent about his wars.

   He was a great organizer, a great builder, and above
all a man of genuine piety, which breathes through all

his inscriptions. When he died, B.C. 562, he was succeeded by his son Evil-Merodach, who reigned only
two years. Then the throne was usurped by a certain
Nergal-sharezer (the son of Bel-zakir-iskun) who had
married the daughter of Nebuchadrezzar. Nergal-
sharezer built himself a new palace and died B.C. 556.
He was followed by his infant son who reigned only
three months, when he was murdered and the throne
seized by Nabonidos (Nabu-nahid), the son of Nebo-
balasu-iqbi, who was not related to the royal family.
Nabonidos was a man of some energy, but he offended
a powerful party in Babylonia by attempting to do
what Hezekiah had done in Jerusalem—centralize the
religious worship of the country and therewith the
political power in the capital. Nabonidos was also an
antiquarian and caused excavations to be made in the
different temples of Babylonia in order to discover
the records of their founders.

We are now well acquainted with the history of
Nabonidos and the fall of his empire, thanks to three
cuneiform documents which have been found in Babylonia. One is an inscription of Nabonidos himself;
another an edict issued by Cyrus shortly after his conquest of the country ; and the third the annals of the
reign of Nabonidos, compiled the year after his over-

throw. The empire of Nabonidos, we learn, extended
as far westward as Gaza, but the ' Manda ' or ' Nomads '
of whom Astyages (Istuvegu) was king had devastated
part of Western Asia and had destroyed the temple
of the Moon-god at Harran. It was not until Cyrus,
'the little servant' of Astyages, had overthrown the
Manda that Nabonidos was able to enter Harran and
rebuild the ruined shrine.

Cyrus and the Fall of Babylon.—Cyrus, like
his fathers, was king of Anzan in Elam, not of Persia.
Anzan had been first occupied, it would appear, by his
great-grandfather Teispes the Achaemenian. The conquest of Astyages and of his capital Ekbatana took
place in B. C. 549, and a year or two later Cyrus
obtained possession of Persia. In B. C. 538 the
population in the south of Babylonia revolted, and
Cyrus entered the country, where he was assisted by
the native party which was hostile to Nabonidos. The
Babylonian army was stationed in northern Babylonia,
but it was utterly defeated at Opis in the month of
Tammuz or June, and on the 14th of the month Sippara opened its gates to the conqueror. Gobryas, the
governor of Kurdistan, was then sent by Cyrus against
Babylon, which also opened its gates 'without fighting,'

THE CYLINDER INSCRIPTION OF CYRUS.

and Nabonidos, who had concealed himself, was taken prisoner. Gobryas placed the temple of Bel under a guard, and the daily services there proceeded as usual. The contract-tablets show that there was equally little cessation of business among the mercantile classes. But it was not until the 3rd of Marchesvan (October) that Cyrus himself arrived in Babylon and proclaimed a general amnesty, which was communicated by Gobryas to 'all the province of Babylon' of which he had been made governor. Shortly afterwards the wife of Nabonidos died; lamentation was made for her throughout Babylonia, and Kambyses, the son of Cyrus, conducted her funeral in one of the Babylonian temples.

Meanwhile Cyrus had assumed the title of 'King of Babylon,' thus claiming to be the legitimate descendant of the ancient Babylonian kings. He announced himself as the devoted worshipper of Bel and Nebo, who by the command of Merodach had overthrown the sacrilegious usurper Nabonidos, and he and his son accordingly offered sacrifices to ten times the usual amount in the Babylonian temples, and restored the images of the gods to their ancient shrines. At the same time he allowed the foreign populations who had been deported to Babylonia to return to their homes along with the statues of their gods. Among these foreign populations, as we know from the Old Testament, were the Jews.

Belshazzar.—One of the sons of Nabonidos was Belshazzar, who is mentioned in the contract-tablets as well as by his father. He seems to have been 'the king's son' who commanded the Babylonian army in its camp near Sippara. If so, it would appear that he had died or been slain before the final invasion of Babylonia by Cyrus, since no reference is made to him on that occasion, and the pretenders who afterwards rose against Darius in Babylonia called themselves not Belshazzar but ' Nebuchadrezzar, the son of Nabonidos.'

Decay of Babylon.—It was after the death of Kambyses and of the Pseudo-Smerdis that these revolts took place in B. C. 521 and 515 (?). The first was a serious one, and was suppressed only after two engagements in the field and a siege of Babylon. The second revolt also needed a long siege for its suppression, and at its conclusion Darius partially destroyed the walls of the city. But in the reign of Xerxes, during the absence of the king in Greece, Babylon revolted again under a certain Samas-erba, who reigned for about a year. On the fall of this champion of Babylonian independence, the temple of Bel, the rallying-place of Babylonian nationality, was in part destroyed. From this time forward the only kings mentioned in the cuneiform tablets are foreigners, Persians, Greeks, and Parthians. The last dated tablet at present known to us is almost as late as the Christian era. It is an astrological text which is dated in the 168th year of Seleucus and the 232nd year of Arsakes, that is to say in B. C. 80.

CHAPTER IV

RELIGION

The religions of Babylonia and Assyria.—
The religion of Assyria was borrowed from that of
Babylonia.   The deities worshipped in the two countries were the same, as also were the ritual and the
religious beliefs of the people.   Almost the only
difference observable in the religion of the two kingdoms was that whereas Bel Merodach was the supreme
god of Babylon, Assur, the impersonation of the old
capital, was the supreme god of Assyria.

**Differences between Babylonian and Assy-
rian religion.**—But the different characters of the
two populations were reflected in their religious con-
ceptions.   The Assyrians were a nation of warriors,
the Babylonians of traders, agriculturists, and scribes.
Assur is accordingly 'a man of war'; it was in re-

liance upon him that the Assyrian armies marched into foreign lands, and compelled their inhabitants to acknowledge him. Not to believe in Assur was a crime, since Assur represented Assyria. Assur, too, admitted no rival at his side : wifeless and childless he stood alone. Once or twice, indeed, an Assyrian scribe ascribes to him a wife or a child, but this is in imitation of Babylonian usage and the belief never took root in Assyria.

Bel-Merodach, on the contrary, was a god of mercy. He is 'the merciful one' who hearkens to those that call upon him and who 'raises the dead to life' through trust in his power. Belat, or Beltis, 'the lady,' stood at his side, a reflection of himself, and the gods were his children who recognized him as their father and creator.

Sumerian religion Shamanistic.—Babylonian religion was a compound of Sumerian and Semitic elements. Sumerian religion had originally been 'Shamanistic' in character. That is to say it had no conception of deities or priests in the usual sense of the words. Each object or force of nature was believed to have its *zi* or 'life' like men and beasts ; the *zi* was a sort of vital principle which caused the

F

arrow to fly, the knife to wound, or the stars to move through the heaven. A personality was given to it, and it thus became what we may term a spirit. With these spirits, accordingly, the sky and earth were peopled; they were in fact as multitudinous as the objects and forces of nature to which they owed their birth. Necessarily the greater number of them were harmful, if not always at any rate at certain times and in certain places. Magical charms alone could protect man from their malevolence or bring down their blessing upon him, and these magical charms and ceremonies were known only to a particular class of persons. To such sorcerer-priests the name of 'shamans' has been assigned, the form of religion represented by them being termed 'Shamanistic.'

Two centres of Babylonian religion.—In prehistoric times two great religious centres existed in Babylonia, from which two divergent streams of religious influence flowed over the country. One of these was Nipur in the north, the other Eridu in the south. Nipur was the seat of Shamanism, and its patron deity in later days still retained the title of Mul-lil or El-lil, 'the lord of the ghost-world.' Eridu, on the other hand, was brought by its trade and situation into contact with foreign culture. It thus became the source of a higher and more spiritual form of faith. The spirit of the water, who had been its special object of adoration, became the culture-god Ea, the lord of the abyss, who is called Oannes in the Greek history of Bêrôssos and was believed to have been the author of Babylonian culture. To him its laws, its arts, and its sciences were alike traced back. Through his wisdom his son Asari-mulu-dugga, ' Asari who benefits mankind,' was enabled to cure the diseases and troubles of men, and teach them how to avoid evil. His teachings were embodied in writing, and so a sacred book grew up, half Bible, half Ritual, which contained hymns to the gods as well as rubrics for the performance of the ceremonies accompanying their recitation.

Under the influence of Eridu the religion of Babylonia ceased to be so purely Shamanistic as it once had been. Certain of the spirits tended to take rank above their fellows and thus to pass into gods. How long this process of development lasted we do not know.

Semitic Influence.—But a time came when the Semites entered the country and were brought into close contact, hostile or peaceable, with its Sumerian inhabitants. The result was a fusion of Sumerian and Semitic religious ideas. An official religion came into existence which consisted of a Semitic form of faith grafted upon a Sumerian root.

The religion of the Semite was essentially different from that of the Sumerian. The primary object of his worship was the Baal, Bel, or ' Lord,' who revealed himself in the sun. Each tribe and each locality had its own Baal; when the tribes coalesced or when the same tribe occupied more than one locality the various Baals were regarded as so many forms of the supreme God.

Each Baal was the father of a family. At his side stood his wife, a colourless reflection of himself, as the wife was of the husband in the Semitic family on earth. Like the father of the family on earth, Baal too in heaven had his children.

Where the religions of the Semite and the Sumerian met and combined, the Sumerian spirits who had emerged above the rest like Ea of Eridu or El-lil of Nipur, were assimilated to the Semitic Baalim. El-lil, in fact, was known throughout the Semitic period as Bel of Nipur. Wherever it was possible a solar character was given to them; in other cases the general characteristics of the Semitic deity were attached to the old Sumerian divinity. The great body of the spirits which had fallen into the background was grouped together as the 300 spirits of heaven (*Igigi*) and the 600 spirits of earth (*Anunnaki*).

The goddess Istar.—In one instance, however, it was the Semite rather than the Sumerian who was affected by the contact between the two forms of faith. The spirit of the evening star became the goddess Istar, who retained her independent position by the side of the male deities. While the other goddesses were absorbed in the persons of their divine consorts like the wife in the Semitic family, Istar, having no consort, remained like the wife in the Sumerian family on a footing of equality with the man. When the name and worship of Istar were passed on to the Semitic peoples of the West, the anomaly led to more than one change in her character. In southern Arabia and Moab she was identified with a male deity ; in Canaan her name received the feminine suffix *-th* (Ashtoreth), and she thus became in large measure an ordinary Semitic goddess.

Bel-Merodach.—After the rise of Babylon as the

capital of the kingdom, its patron-god Merodach
became the supreme Baal or Bel of Babylonia. He
had already been identified with Asari-mulu-dugga,
the son of Ea, and the attributes of the latter were
accordingly transferred to the new Bel. It was to
him that the great temple of Ê-Saggil was erected in
Babylon, while the interpreter of his will to men,
Nebo, the divine 'prophet,' had his temple Ê-Zida in
the neighbouring suburb of Borsippa. At Nipur
a god whose name has been variously read Uras,
Nin-ip, Bar and Adar, but the true pronunciation of
which is still unknown, stood in much the same
relation to El-lil that Nebo did to Merodach. He
was, however, regarded as a solar warrior instead of
as a prophet.

Other deities.—Nergal was worshipped in Kutha
and its cemeteries; Samas, 'the Sun,' at Sippara;
Sin, 'the Moon,' at Ur and Harran; Anu, 'the Sky,'
at Erech, where he was associated with Istar. Along
with Ea and Bel of Nipur, Anu formed a triad which
represented in the official religion the three elementary
deities of the sea, the earth, and the heavens. The
sea, however, was rather the primordial 'deep' out of
which all things arose than the sea of the actual

world, while 'the heaven of Anu' was beyond the
visible sky, and Bel was the prince of the air and the
underworld.

WINGED BULL OR HOUSE-GUARDIAN.

Sacred books and ritual.—Along with the
growth of the official religion went the growth and
completion of the Chaldaean Bible and Prayer-book.
The festivals of the gods were numerous; the ceremonies to be performed by the priests were more

numerous still.   The ceremonies were usually accompanied by the recitation of one or more hymns; these
hymns were written in Sumerian, which had now
become the sacred language of Chaldaea just as Latin
is the sacred language of the Roman Church, and
since Sumerian was no longer understood by the
majority of the people they were provided with interlinear translations into Semitic Babylonian.   From
time to time the pronunciation of the old Sumerian
words was indicated, for just as it was needful that
the inspired words should be handed down without
the slightest alteration, so also was it needful that
they should be pronounced aright.   An error even in
pronunciation was supposed to invalidate the cere-
mony.   Among the hymns is a collection of penitential psalms of which the following lines will give some
idea :—

'O lord, my sins are many, my transgressions are great!
 O my god, my sins are many, my transgressions are great!
 O my goddess, my sins are many, my transgressions are great!

      .   .   .   .

The lord in the wrath of his heart has regarded me ;
God in the fierceness of his heart has revealed himself to me.
The goddess has been violent against me, and has put me to
     grief.

      .   .   .   .

I sought for help and none took my hand;

I wept and none stood at my side;
I cried aloud and there was none that heard me.
To my god, the merciful one, I turn myself, I utter my
    prayer.
    .   .   .   .

O my god, seven times seven are my transgressions: forgive
    my sins!'

The Priests.—The existence of a hierarchy of
gods, of a Bible, and of a Prayer-book implies the
existence of a priesthood. The sorcerer of prehistoric
times became the priest of later Babylonia. The
priests were distinguished into several classes. At
the head came the High-priest who was often the
monarch; in Assyria indeed this was commonly the
case. Subordinate to him were other high-priests,
and under them again the 'anointers' (who cleansed
the sacred vessels of the sanctuary), the priests of
Istar and the 'elders.' By the side of them stood
the 'prophets' (*asipi*) under a 'chief.' The prophets
could predict the future and were consulted on
matters of state. We hear of armies being accompanied by them into the field, and when Assur-bani-
pal suppressed the revolt of the Babylonians 'by the
command of the prophets,' he says, 'I purified their
shrines and cleansed their chief places of prayer.
The angry gods and wrathful goddesses I soothed

with supplications and penitential psalms. I restored and established in peace their daily sacrifices which they had discontinued.'

The Temples.—The temples were provided with towers which served for the observation of the stars, and stood within large courts. In the shrine was a ' mercy-seat' whereon the god 'seated himself' on certain occasions. At Balawât near Nineveh the mercy-seat had the form of a coffer or ark, in which two written tables of stone were placed. In front of it stood the altar approached by steps. In the court was a 'sea' or large basin of water, which like that of Solomon was, in one case at all events, supported on bulls of bronze. The images of the gods were almost invariably of human form.

Astro-theology.—The prominence given to the study of astronomy had much to do with giving Babylonian religion an astral character. The stars were worshipped ; Istar herself was originally the evening star, and most of the principal deities were identified with the planets and chief fixed stars. The importance of the stars for the regulation of the calendar, moreover, kept them constantly before the eyes of the priests. But whether Babylonian astro-theology was not really primitive or whether it went back to the pre-Semitic period we do not yet know.

Sacrifices and offerings.—Sacrifices were offered to the stars, as to the other divinities. Besides the sacrifices, offerings were also made of meal, dates, oil, and wine. The sacrifices and offerings must have been numerous since in the larger temples there was not only 'the daily sacrifice' but also constant services both by day and night. On the great festivals, moreover, there were services of a special character, as also when days of thanksgiving or humiliation were ordained. The sacrifices and offerings were provided partly by endowments, partly by voluntary gifts (sometimes called *kurbanni*, the Hebrew *korban*), partly by obligatory contributions, the most important of which were the 'tithes.'

The Sabbath.—Besides the festivals of the gods there was a *sabattu* or 'Sabbath,' observed on the 9th, 14th, 19th, 21st, and 28th day of the month, on which various kinds of work were forbidden to be done. Food even was not allowed to be cooked, or medicine to be taken. The *sabattu* is described as 'a day of rest for the heart,' and a 'free-will offering' had to be made in the night of it.

Monotheistic tendency.—Among the educated classes religious feeling seems to have been fervent, and at times the language used approaches that of monotheism. Thus in an early hymn to the Moon-god which was composed in the city of Ur, we read:—

‘ Father, long-suffering and full of forgiveness, whose hand up-
   holds the life of all mankind ! . . .
 First-born, omnipotent, whose heart is immensity, and there is
   none who may fathom it ! . . .
 In heaven, who is supreme ?   Thou alone, thou art supreme !
 On earth, who is supreme ?   Thou alone, thou art supreme ! ’

So, again, Nebuchadrezzar prays as follows to Bel-Merodach :—

‘ O prince, thou art from everlasting, lord of all that exists, for the king whom thou lovest, whom thou callest by name, as it seems good to thee, thou guidest his name aright, thou watchest over him in the path of righteousness. I, the prince who obeys thee, am the work of thy hands ; thou hast created me and hast entrusted to me the sovereignty over multitudes of men, according to thy goodness, O lord, which thou hast made to pass over them all. Let me love thy supreme lordship, let the fear of thy divinity exist in my heart, and give what seemeth good to thee, since thou maintainest my life.’

The future life.—The mass of the people, however, were sunk in the grossest superstition, and the future to which they looked forward was sufficiently dreary. Hades lay beneath the earth, where the spirits of the dead flitted about like bats in darkness with dust only for their food. A happier lot was reserved for the few, and a prayer is made for an Assyrian king that after death he should ascend to 'the land of the silver sky.'

Cosmology.—In early Sumerian days the heaven was believed to rest on the peak of 'the mountain of the world,' in the far north-east, where the gods had their habitations (cf. Isa. xiv. 13), while an ocean or 'deep' encircled the earth which rested upon its surface. With the progress of knowledge truer ideas of geography came to prevail. The later cosmogony is represented in the first tablet of the Creation story where the old gods are resolved into cosmical elements. The 'deep' is said to have been 'the generator' of the heavens and the earth, 'Mummu-Tiamat' (the chaos of the sea) being 'the mother of them all. . . . At that time the gods had not appeared. . . . Then the [great] gods were created, Lakhmu and Lakhamu issued forth the first.' Next came the creation of An-sar and Ki-sar, 'the upper' and 'lower firmament,' who in their turn gave birth to Anu, Ea, and Bel. The struggle between Merodach, the god of light and order, with Tiamat, the dragon of darkness, chaos, and evil, occupied a prominent place in the Epic of the Creation. Along with Tiamat there were ranged in battle the evil creatures of night and destruction, most of whom had composite forms. The belief in them had been inherited from the age of Shamanism, and they were regarded as the products of a first and imperfect creation. Some of them came to symbolize the powers of darkness, others were transported to the skies, certain of the allies of Tiamat being the Zodiacal animals, while out of the skin of Tiamat Merodach constructed the heaven itself. In the Epic Tiamat is identified with the source of the fountains of the great deep.

CHAPTER V

Aids to the reading of the texts.—The origin
of the cuneiform system of writing has been already
described, as well as its chief peculiarities. We must
now say something about the causes which have led
to our being able to read an ordinary Assyrian text
almost as easily as a page of the Old Testament.

(1) The 'determinatives' have already been mentioned which define so many words and names.
(2) The ideographs often prove a great assistance, as
words of unknown meaning interchange with ideographs the signification of which is already known.
(3) The fact that the characters express syllables
gives us the precise pronunciation of the words, and
so enables us to read them with a certainty which is
impossible in Hebrew or Phoenician where the

vowels are not denoted in writing. (4) Assyrian is a Semitic language, and the Semitic languages are as closely related to one another as are the Romanic languages (French, Italian, Spanish, &c.) in modern Europe. Consequently most of the words and grammatical forms found in Assyrian recur in one or other of the Semitic idioms. (5) But above all, the Assyrian scribes themselves have provided us with the most abundant materials for interpreting the inscriptions.

The libraries.—The amount of Assyro-Babylonian literature already known is very large. If all the texts at present in the museums of Europe and America could be published, they would rival in extent the books of the Old Testament. Most of the texts are on tablets of clay and have come from the libraries of Nineveh and Babylonia. Every great Babylonian city had at least one library, and the Assyrian kings established other libraries in their own country in imitation of those of Babylonia. About two-thirds of the library of Nineveh, which was largely the creation of Assur-bani-pal, is now in the British Museum. Scribes were kept constantly at work there copying and re-editing old texts, and sometimes writing new ones. A considerable proportion of the texts was brought from Babylonia : a colophon attached to each tablet usually states from what library the text had originally come. The texts were carefully edited ; when there was a lacuna in the original the scribe tells us so, and whether it was old or recent ; also if the Babylonian character were one which he did not recognize he confesses that he could not read it. Besides the clay tablets, the libraries contained papyri which have now perished.

Varieties of literature.—The texts related to all the branches of knowledge studied at the time. Astronomy and astrology, mathematics, geography, medicine, law, history, religion, and mythology, private and public correspondence, mercantile transactions, political documents, the pseudo-science of omens, lists of beasts, birds, vegetables, and stones, are all represented in it, and last, but not least, philology. The necessity of translating and explaining the Sumerian texts doubtless gave philology so prominent a place. Under the head of philology come interlinear and parallel translations of Sumerian documents, together with commentaries and exercises, reading-books and grammars of the two languages,

G

endless lists of characters with their phonetic values and significations, and numerous vocabularies partly bilingual, partly containing catalogues of Semitic synonyms. The decipherer thus has at his command a most elaborate system for learning the Assyrian and Sumerian languages compiled by the Assyrians themselves. Time after time the signification of a new word is given by its synonym or synonyms in the lexical lists, and words of uncertain meaning in Hebrew have more than once been settled by means of their Assyrian equivalents.

The texts autotypes.—The cuneiform texts further possess an advantage of which the student of the Old and New Testament Scriptures might well be envious. They are the autotypes of the scribes who wrote them for the libraries in the ruins of which they have been found. The texts have never passed through the hands of later copyists little acquainted with the language in which they were composed. The corruptions of the text, such as they are, go back to the scribes of Assur-bani-pal or Nebucha-drezzar, in some cases to the scribes even of the pre-Semitic period.

Astronomy.—The great work on astronomy and

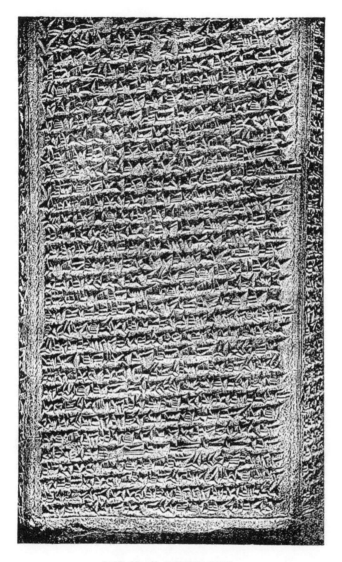

PART OF AN ASSYRIAN BOOK.

astrology in seventy-two chapters or books was originally compiled for the library of Sargon of Accad. It contained chapters on the eclipses or conjunction of the sun and moon, on the planets, the fixed stars, and the comets, and proves that observations of the heavens had been made for a long while previous to its composition. The path of the sun through the signs of the Zodiac had already been mapped out: in fact the Zodiacal Signs owe their origin to the astronomers of Babylonia. At the time they were first named the vernal equinox began with Taurus.

Mathematics.—Among the mathematical treatises may be mentioned tables of cube and square roots from the library of Senkereh. The Babylonian system of notation resembled that of the Romans, but by an ingenious application of the sexagesimal system high numbers could be expressed in a very small number of figures.

Medicine and law. — The standard work on medicine was voluminous like that on astronomy. It contained a vast number of prescriptions for different diseases, which read very much like modern ones. Law occupied a large space in Babylonian and

Assyrian life, and codes of law, which protected the
slave as well as the woman, went back to Sumerian
times.   A considerable part of the law was based
on cases which had already been decided by the
judges.   The judges were appointed by the king,
and, at all events in a later age, were under a presi-
dent.   Important cases were heard before several
judges at once; thus a case which was tried at
Babylon in B. C. 547 was heard before six judges
and registered by their two clerks.

History and mythology.—Historical documents
are numerous and include the lists of Assyrian epo-
nyms, after whom the successive years were named,
as well as of the dynasties of kings and the number
of years each king reigned.   Religious literature,
however, was still more largely represented.   As has
been stated, a considerable portion of it consisted
of hymns to the gods, psalms, and ritual texts.   But
there were also lists of the multitudinous deities and
their temples, and more especially religious myths
and legends.   One of these described the visit of
the goddess Istar to Hades in search of her dead
husband Tammuz, the Sun-god, and told how she
left some of her adornment at each of its seven gates,

until at last she stood stripped and bare before the mistress of the Underworld, where the waters of life gush forth. In another the adventures of the first man Adapa are related, and how he was summoned to heaven to answer the charge of having broken the wings of the south-wind. We possess two fragments of this myth, the earlier part being written on a broken tablet which was found in the library of Nineveh, while the latter part of it has been found on one of the cuneiform documents discovered at Tel el-Amarna in Egypt, where it had been copied for Egyptian or Canaanite students some eight centuries before the library of Nineveh was in existence.

The Chaldaean epic and the Deluge.—One of the most famous of the legends is the Chaldaean account of the Deluge, which was discovered by George Smith in 1872. Its close resemblance to the Biblical account of the same event is well known. It embodied at least two earlier versions of the story, and in its present form is inserted as an episode in the great Epic of the Babylonian hero Gilgames. The Epic was composed by a certain Sin-liqi-unnini in twelve books, and was arranged on an astronomical principle, the subject of each book corresponding with the name of a Zodiacal sign. Thus the account of the Deluge is introduced into the eleventh book, which answers to Aquarius the eleventh sign of the Zodiac.

Gilgames, it was said, was the fated child of whom it had been prophesied that he would slay his grandfather. Though his mother had been confined in a tower, he was nevertheless born and conveyed to safety on the wings of an eagle. When grown to man's estate he saved Erech from the enemy and made it the seat of his dominion. He overthrew Khumbaba the tyrant of the forest of cedars, and found a friend and guide in the satyr Ea-bani. The goddess Istar wooed him in marriage, but he reproached her with the woes she had already brought on her hapless lovers and scorned her beauty. In revenge she besought Anu, her father, to create a winged bull, which should attack the hero. Gilgames, however, slew the bull and returned in triumph to Erech with his spoils. But misfortune fell upon him. Ea-bani was killed by the bite of a gad-fly, his soul rising up from the ground to the heaven of heroes, and Gilgames himself was smitten with a sore disease. To heal it he sailed beyond the mouth of the Euphrates and the river of death, and here conversed with Xisuthrus, the Chaldaean Noah, who, like Enoch, had been translated without seeing death. Xisuthrus told him the story of the Deluge, and instructed him how to cure his malady.

Epic of the Creation.—The Assyrian Epic of the Creation, the discovery of which was also due to George Smith, has already been alluded to. Its parallelism with the account of the Creation, in the first chapter of Genesis, was noticed from the first. The first tablet opens with a description of the deep or watery chaos, while the fifth tablet describes the appointment of the heavenly bodies for signs and for seasons, and in the seventh comes an account of the creation of the animals. The second and third tablets, however, and possibly the fourth, were occupied with the story of the struggle between Tiamat the dragon of darkness, and Merodach the Sun-god, which finds its echo in the Apocalypse (Rev. xii. 7–9). Out of the skin of Tiamat, Merodach formed the firmament which 'divided the waters which were under the firmament from the waters which were above it.' Other accounts of the Creation existed, which differed essentially from that of the Epic. Thus there was one that was written for the Library of Kutha and described an imperfect creation which foreshadowed as it were the present one. Mr. Pinches, again, has discovered a Sumerian legend of the origin of things which seems to have been current at Eridu. But in the Epic a considerable number of the older cosmological legends were embodied and combined, and a gloss of materialistic philosophy put upon them. It is this gloss which makes it difficult to believe that the Epic can be of much antiquity. The materials of which it is composed doubtless go back to an early period, but in its present form it belongs to an age when the deities of the old faith were resolved into philosophical abstractions and the forces of nature. At present, at all events, we have no reasons for thinking that it is earlier than the time of the Second Assyrian Empire.

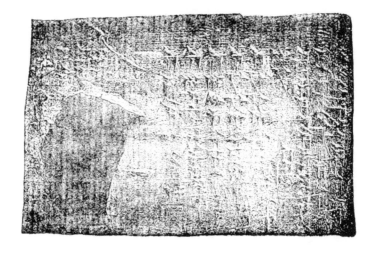

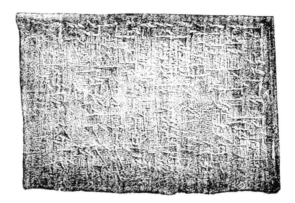

CONTRACT-TABLETS.

CHAPTER VI

SOCIAL LIFE

The Contract-tablets.—We have learnt a great deal about the social life of Babylonia and Assyria from the contract-tablets which have been found in enormous numbers in Babylonia. A few have also come from the library of Nineveh, relating for the most part to the sale and lease of house property. Some of them have Aramaic dockets attached to them, giving the names of the persons mentioned in the contract and the nature of its contents. These dockets serve to verify the method of cuneiform decipherment, and are an indication that in the time of Tiglath-pileser III and his successors Aramaic was the common language of trade.

Some of the Babylonian contract-tablets go back to the time of Khammurabi and his dynasty, and are in

Sumerian. But the larger number are of much later date, and extend from the reign of Kandalanu, the predecessor of Nabopolassar, to that of Xerxes. For many years we have a continuous series of documents dated month by month in each year. A contract-tablet was often enclosed in an envelope of clay, on which its principal contents were inscribed. They were kept in large jars which answered to our modern safes.

Married Life.—From the contracts relating to matrimony we learn that polygamy was very rare, and that the wife enjoyed a considerable amount of independence. The dowry she brought with her on marriage had to be restored to her in case of divorce. Moreover the woman could act apart from her husband, entering into partnership, trading with her money and conducting law-suits in her own name. In B. C. 555 we find a father transferring all his property to his daughter, and reserving only the use of it during the rest of his life. On the other hand wives, like concubines, could sometimes be purchased, though in this case if the husband married again he stipulated that he would send his first wife back to her home along with a certain sum of money. Children could be adopted, and there was the utmost freedom as regards the devolution of property, which could be 'tied up' by will.

Burial.—The dead were buried after complete or partial cremation. With the exception of the kings they were interred in cemeteries outside the towns, tombs and tombstones being erected over them, with rivulets, which symbolized 'the water of life,' flowing at their side.

Slavery.—Slavery was an ancient institution, but the slave was protected by law as far back as the Sumerian period. In later times he could even appear as party to a suit, and could recover his freedom by manumission, by purchase, by proving that he had been unlawfully enslaved, or by his adoption into the family of a citizen. Slaves could be impressed into the royal service, so that in selling a slave it was usual to stipulate that the seller should be responsible for any trouble arising from such a cause. Poor parents sometimes sold their children into slavery, and the Sumerian law ordered a son who denied his father to be shorn and sold as a slave.

Lowness of Wages.—Few persons were so poor as not to be able to keep one slave at least. But the

existence of slavery caused wages to be low, and
lowered the character and position of the free labourer.
Thus we find that a skilled labourer, like a copper-
smith, received only six *qas* (about 8½ quarts) of flour
for overlaying a chariot with a lining of copper, and
that only 1*s.* 6*d.* was paid for painting the stucco of
a wall.

Property.—The tenure of a farm was of various
kinds. Sometimes the property belonged half to the
landlord, half to the tenant, the tenant doing all the
work and handing the landlord's half of the produce
to his agent. Sometimes while the tenant gave his
work, the landlord provided him with carts, oxen, and
other necessaries. At other times the tenant received
only a third, a fourth, or even a tenth of the produce,
besides paying a fixed rent of two-thirds of the dates
gathered from the palms on the estate. The landlord
could dismiss the tenant, who was also required to
build the farm house if one did not already exist.

When house property or land was let or sold it was
minutely described, and numerous witnesses to the
deed of sale or lease were required. The length of
the lease as well as the rent had to be stated, any
transgression of the terms of the lease being punished

with a severe fine. The tenant had to return the property in the state in which he found it. The rent of course depended on the size and value of the property, and could be paid half-yearly as well as three times a year. Houses, further, might be bought and sold through the intervention of an agent.

Taxes.—Taxation was probably heavy. In the time of Sennacherib, Nineveh had to pay the treasury 30 talents a year, while Carchemish was assessed at 100 talents. Taxes were also levied in kind, and there was an *octroi* duty upon goods entering the town. The metal,—gold, silver, and bronze,—was measured out by weight, a coinage not making its appearance until late in Babylonian history, though, as in Egypt, rings of gold or silver, which took the place of coins, were used at an early time.

Prices.—The value of grain and dates necessarily varied from time to time. Under Nebuchadrezzar, the quart of sesame cost a little over a penny, in the twelfth year of Nabonidos it was a little less than $1\frac{1}{2}d$. In the seventh year of Nebuchadrezzar dates were about a halfpenny a quart, in his thirty-eighth year the quart was only $\frac{1}{25}$ of a penny. In the reign of Cambyses a quart of corn cost $2\frac{1}{2}d$.

H

The prices of other things were higher. In the reign of Darius a lady sold 200 sheep for £135, in that of Nebuchadrezzar an ox, sacrificed in the temple of the Sun-god at Sippara, cost £2. We hear of asses sold for £7 10s., and £2, and of five casks of wine purchased for £1 10s.

Usury.—Deeds of partnership are common ; so also are deeds relating to money-lending. The usurer, in fact, was a prominent person in the trading community of Babylonia. Under Nebuchadrezzar and his successors the usual rate of interest was 20 per cent., the interest being paid each month, though we also hear of $13\frac{1}{3}$ per cent. In concluding a bargain, it was usually stipulated that if the money were not paid by a specified date, interest should be paid upon it until it was paid in full.

The Army.—By the side of the commercial class stood a numerous body of military and civil officials. At the head of the Assyrian army was the Tartan (*turtannu*) or Commander-in-chief, and under him came a large staff of officers. The army itself was highly organized. In addition to the infantry and cavalry there were numerous chariots, in one of which the king rode when he commanded in person. In the time of Tiglath-pileser III, saddles, leathern drawers, and high boots were introduced for the cavalry, and a corps of slingers and pioneers was created by Sennacherib. The infantry were divided into heavy-armed and light-armed, many of the heavy-armed wearing coats of mail formed of metal scales sewn to a leather shirt. Helmets were largely used, as well as shields. The army carried with it on the march various engines for attacking the walls of a town—battering-rams, ladders, crow-bars, and the like —as well as tents. The royal tent was accompanied by a cooking and a dining-tent, and was elaborately furnished. We learn from the contract-tablets, that in the reign of Nabonidos, rather more than $2\frac{1}{2}$ bushels of wheat were furnished to each of the bowmen, while 54 *qas* (75 quarts) of beer were provided on a particular day, 'for the troops which had marched from Babylon.'

Navy.—A fleet was kept in Babylonia, and the king had a State-barge on the Euphrates. The Assyrians, however, were not a naval people, and the biremes, employed by Sennacherib when he attacked the Chaldaean colony in the Persian Gulf, were built and manned by Phoenicians.

The Bureaucracy.—The prefects or satraps of the Assyrian provinces and subject cities were appointed by the king, like the military officers, and were responsible to him. A certain number of them were eligible for the post of *limmu,* or eponym, after whom the year was named—an honour which they shared with the monarch. The office does not appear to have existed in Babylonia.

Among the tablets which have come from the library of Nineveh are some which contain long lists of Assyrian officials. They were a very numerous body, but we need mention only the Rab-shakeh (*Rab-saki*), 'chief of the princes,' or Vizier, the Rab-saris (*Rab-sa-resi*) or 'chief of the nobles,' and the Rab-mag (*Rab-mugi*) or 'chief physician.' The identification of the two last is due to Mr. Pinches.

The priests and judges have already been alluded to, as also the clerks or scribes, many of whom, at least in Babylonia, were also priests. Poets and musicians were attached to the court, and we hear of a grant of land being made to a court-poet, in Babylonia, for some verses in which he had doubtless flattered the king. Society, in short, was highly organized, and the principle of a subdivision of labour was fully understood.

In one important respect, however, the basis upon which society rested in Babylonia and in Assyria was different. The government of Babylonia was theocratic, that of Assyria was military. While Assyria with its bureaucratic centralization is an anticipation of imperial Rome, Babylonia with its theocratic constitution is an anticipation of papal Rome. The king was the adopted son of Bel, and his right to rule was based on the fact that Bel, the true lord and ruler of the State, had delegated to him his power.

APPENDIX

—+—

The silver shekel was worth about 3s.

[1] As determined by Dr. Oppert.

[2] Capitals denote that the Semitic pronunciation of the ideograph is unknown.

THE MONTHS OF THE YEAR.

Assyrian Name.	Sumerian Name.	Zodiacal Sign.	Corresponding Months.
(1) Nisannu (Nisan)	Month of 'the dweller in the Asherah¹'	Aries	March-April.
(2) Aaru (Iyyar)	'The directing bull'	Taurus	April-May.
(3) Sivanu (Sivan)	'Bricks' (?)	Gemini	May-June.
(4) Duzu (Tammuz)	'The growth of seed'	Cancer	June-July.
(5) Abu (Ab)	'The fiery-hot'	Leo	July-August.
(6) Ululu (Elul)	'The message of Istar'	Virgo	August-September.
(7) Tasritu (Tisri)	'The holy mound'	Libra	September-October.
(8) Arakh-savna (Marchesvan, 'the eighth month')	'Opposite the foundation' (of the year)	Scorpio	October-November.
(9) Kisilivu (Chisleu)	'The cloudy'	Sagittarius	November-December.
(10) Dhabitu (Tebet)	'The cave of the dawn' (?)	Capricornus	December-January.
(11) Sabadhu (Sebat)	'The curse of rain'	Aquarius	January-February.
(12) Addaru (Adar)	The month of 'cultivation'	Pisces	February-March.
(13) Arakh-makhru (Ve-Adar), the intercalary month.			

¹ *Zaggara*, rendered by the Semitic *bit ili* (Beth-el), 'house of God,' as well as by *asirtu*, 'the symbol of the goddess Asherah' (mistranslated 'grove' in the Authorized Version of the Old Testament).

BABYLONIAN KINGS.

B.C.

Sargon of Akkad 3800

Naram-Sin his son 3700

(1) The Dynasty of Babylon : 11 kings for
 304 years 2478–2174
 The sixth king of the dynasty was Khammurabi 2356–2301

(2) The Dynasty of Lagas : 11 kings for
 368 years 2174–1806

(3) The Kassite Dynasty : 36 kings for
 576 years 9 months . . . 1806–1229
 Among the kings of this dynasty were Burna-
buryas (cir. B.C. 1420), the contemporary of
the Egyptian Pharaohs Amenophis III and
Amenophis IV, and Kuri-galzu (cir. B. C. 1400).
The last six kings were :
 Rimmon-nadin-suma 1297
 Conquest of Babylon by Tiglath-Uras of
 Assyria 1291
 Expulsion of the Assyrians ; Rimmon-
 suma-natsir king 1284
 Meli-sipak 1261
 Merodach-baladan I 1246
 Zamama-nadin-sumi 1233
 Bel-suma-nadin 1232

(4) The Dynasty of Isin : 11 kings for 72
 years 6 months 1229–1156

B. C.

(5) The Dynasty of the Sea-coast : 3 kings
     for 21 years 5 months .   .   . 1156–1135
(6) The Dynasty of Bit-Bazi : 3 kings for 20
     years 3 months   .   .   . 1135–1115
(7) An Elamite usurper for 6 years.   . 1115–1109
(8) The 31 [kings] of the Dynasty of
     Babylon 1109– 730
   Among them were :
     Nebuchadrezzar I .   .   . 1109–1096
     Merodach-nadin-akhi   .   . 1096–1090
     Merodach-sapik-zirrat   .   . cir. 1075
     Nebo-baladan   .   .   . cir. 880
     Merodach-balasu-iqbi   .   . cir. 820
     Nabu-natsir (Nabonassar)   .   . 747
     Nabu-nadin-ziri (Nadios) his son . 733
     Nabu-suma-yukin his son   .   . 731
(9) The Dynasty of Sape : Yukin-zira (Chin-
     ziros)   730
(10) The Assyrian Dynasties :
     Pulu (Pul, Pôros), called Tiglath-pileser
     III in Assyria   727
     Ululâ, called Shalmaneser IV in Assyria . 725
     Merodach-baladan II, the Chaldaean from
     the Sea-coast   721
     Sargon of Assyria 709
     Sennacherib his son   .   .   . 704

[1] The fracture of the tablet makes the arrangement of this
Dynasty not absolutely certain.

Sogdianos, his half-brother, for seven   B.C.
   months 425
Dareios II, Nothos (or Okhos) his brother 424
Artaxerxes II (Mnêmôn) his son . . 405
Okhos (Uvasu) the son of Artaxerxes . 362
Arses his son 339
Dareios III, Kodomannos . . . 336
Conquered by Alexander the Great . . 330

ASSYRIAN KINGS.
Sargon asserts he was preceded by 330 Assyrian kings.

HIGH PRIESTS OF ASSUR.

Isme-Dagon . . . . . . cir. 1850
Samas-Rimmon I his son 1820
           *   *   *
Igur-Kapkapu . . . . . . ?
Samas-Rimmon II his brother . . . ?
           *   *   *
Khallu . . . . ?
Irisum his son . . . . . . ?

KINGS OF ASSYRIA.

Bel-Kapkapu 'the founder of the monarchy' . ?
           *   *   *
Ada'si . . . . ?
Bel-basi his son . . . . . . ?
        *   *   *

	B. C.
Assur-bil-nisi-su	cir. 1450
Buzur-Assur	. 1440
Assur-nadin-akhi	. 1420
Assur-yuballidh his son	. 1400
Bel-nirari his son	. 1380
Pudilu (Pedael) his son	. 1360
Rimmon-nirari I his son . . .	. 1340
Shalmaneser I his son (founder of Calah)	. 1320
Tiglath-Uras I his son	. 1300
Assur-natsir-pal I his son . . .	. 1280
Assur-narara	. 1270
Nebo-dân his son	. 1265

*   *   *

Bel-kudurri-utsur	. 1230
Uras-pileser	. 1215
Assur-dân I his son	. 1185
Mutaggil-Nebo his son	. 1160
Assur-ris-ilim his son	. 1140
Tiglath-pileser I his son	. 1115
Assur-bil-kala his son	. 1090
Samas-Rimmon I his brother . . .	. 1070

*   *   *

Assur-irbi	. ?

*   *   *

Tiglath-pileser II	. 950
Assur-dân II his son	. 930
Rimmon-nirari II his son . . .	B. C. 911
Tiglath-Uras II his son	. 889
Assur-natsir-pal II his son . . .	. 883

B. C.

Shalmaneser II his son	858
Assur-dain-pal (Sardanapallos), rebel-king .	825
Samas-Rimmon II his brother . . .	823
Rimmon-nirari III his son	810
Shalmaneser III	781
Assur-dân III	771
Assur-nirari	753
Tiglath-pileser III, Pulu (Pul, Pôros), usurper.	745
Shalmaneser IV, Ululâ, usurper . . .	727
Sargon usurper	722
Sennacherib (Sin-akhi-erba) his son . .	705
Esar-haddon I (Assur-akhi-iddina) his son .	681
Assur-bani-pal (Sardanapallos) his son . .	668
Assur-etil-ilani-yukinni his son . . .	?
Sin-sarra-iskuñ (Sarakos)	?
Destruction of Nineveh	606

SYNCHRONISMS BETWEEN ASSYRIAN AND BIBLICAL
HISTORY.

B. C.

Battle of Qarqar; Shalmaneser II defeats
Hadadezer of Damascus, Ahab of
Israel, &c. 853
Campaigns against Hadadezer of Damascus 850–845
Campaign against Hazael of Damascus; tribute
paid to Shalmaneser by Jehu 'the son
of Omri' 841

THE PRINCIPAL DEITIES OF BABYLONIA AND
ASSYRIA.

Anu (Sumerian Ana), the sky-god of Erech, and wife
　　Anat

Bel the elder (Sum. Mul-lil or El-lil), the earth-god of
　　Nipur, and wife Beltis.

Ea, the water-god of Eridu, and wife Dav-kina.

Bel-Merodach (Maruduk) of Babylon, the son of Ea,
　　and wife Zarpanit.

Istar, the goddess of the evening-star, the daughter of
　　Sin.

Sin, the Moon-god of Ur, the son of Bel of Nipur.

Samas, the Sun-god, the son of Sin; also called Â.

Rimmon (Rammanu) or Barqu (Sum. Mer), the air-
　　god.

Uras [1], the warrior-god of Nipur, the minister of the
　　elder Bel.

Nebo (Nabu), 'the prophet' of Borsippa, the minister
　　of Merodach.

Tasmit, 'the hearer,' the wife of Nebo.

Nusku, a Sumerian deity identified with Nebo.

Nergal, the warrior-god of Kutha.

Assur, the national-god of Assyria.

[1] The reading of the name of this god is doubtful. It has
been variously transcribed Bar, Nin-ip, and Adar, the last of
which, however, is certainly wrong.

Oxford
HORACE HART, PRINTER TO THE UNIVERSITY

For EU product safety concerns, contact us at Calle de José Abascal, 56–1°,
28003 Madrid, Spain or eugpsr@cambridge.org.

www.ingramcontent.com/pod-product-compliance
Ingram Content Group UK Ltd.
Pitfield, Milton Keynes, MK11 3LW, UK
UKHW012338130625
459647UK00009B/370